# Livin' Lahaina Loca

JoAnn Bassett

First published by JoAnn Bassett
Green Valley, AZ 85614
http:www.joannbassett.com

ISBN: 1-4750-7106-X
ISBN-13: 9781475071061

This book is a work of fiction. Places, events, and situations in this book are purely fictional and any resemblance to actual persons, living or dead, is coincidental.

Printed in the United States of America

Also by JoAnn Bassett:

MAI TAI BUTTERFLY
MAUI WIDOW WALTZ,
The First book in the "Islands of Aloha Mystery" series

Discover the latest titles by JoAnn Bassett at http://www.joannbassett.com

For my son, Tommy, an RSDW kind of guy.

# 1

A fat rubbery hand glommed onto my left breast. I whirled around and came nose-to-nose with a plastic mask sporting an impish grin and saucer-sized black ears. Halloween night in Lahaina, Maui. The happiest place on earth for a cartoon mouse looking to cop a feel.

"You don't wanna go there," I said, grabbing the groper's forearm just above the white four-fingered glove. The reveler didn't release his grip so I clamped down even harder, squeezing the radius bone against the ulna. Then I jerked the arm down—fast. For a split second I considered giving it a quick twist to pop it out of the elbow joint, but didn't. After all, this masked goon could be an inebriated friend or colleague. Nothing's sacred after seven or eight beers.

I let go and the lecherous mouse skittered away as fast as the swirling crowd would allow. I resumed my upstream trek to the Lahaina Yacht Club.

Before I go into why I'd come to Lahaina Town on the craziest, most crowded night of the year, I think I should introduce myself. My chosen name is Pali Moon. The name on my birth certificate is something else, but only a few people would put that name to this face so I just stick with Pali. On the mainland my name would be spelled *Polly*—but most of us born and raised in the islands usually prefer the Hawaiian spelling. Makes us feel special—even ethnic—but I'm far from meeting most folks' image of a native Hawaiian. I've got light eyes and light hair. And

I'm no *ali'i* princess—you know, the gals with the girth. I'm a standard five six and about one-twenty-five, give or take.

That Halloween night I'd come to town on business. A bad night for conducting any kind of business—except maybe monkey—but I had no choice. A bridesmaid had gone missing the night before at a bachelorette party and no one had seen or heard from her for an entire day. Since I was the wedding planner in charge, I felt it was my responsibility to track her down and bring her back to the fold. She was young, gorgeous, and well-endowed. I only hoped she hadn't gone and trumped the bride by having her own quickie nuptials with some squinty-eyed yachtsman who'd come to Maui for Halloween—the Mardi Gras of the Pacific.

I pushed through the saloon-type doors of the yacht club and was immediately greeted with a sign warning this was a PRIVATE club. It was restricted, but not upscale. The ancient wood floors creaked underfoot, and the funky décor was right out of the mid-eighties. The ceiling was festooned with hundreds of burgees—those colorful little flags that the well-heeled fly from the back of their boat to let you know which snooty yacht club they belong to.

"You a member?" The bouncer guarding the door ran it all together, so it sounded like *remember?* It took me a second to consider what it was I might have forgotten.

"No, I'm here on a mission."

He eyed me as if I was about to hit him up for the United Way.

"I'm a local wedding planner," I said. "I'm looking for one of the girls in the wedding party."

*Local* is a magic word around here. *Local* gets you substantial discounts, warnings instead of speeding tickets, and assistance instead of a shrug. We even have a word for it: *kama'aina*. It's kind of like a secret handshake.

"You think she's here?" He eyed the shoulder-to-shoulder crowd on the groaning wooden deck jutting out over the water. Personally, I wouldn't take my chances on a jammed lanai held up by timber pilings that have been marinating in salt water for forty years, no matter how great the sunset view. But that's just me.

"I don't know. I was hoping maybe you'd recall seeing her when she came in. She doesn't exactly 'blend.' You know, born a few decades too late to be a Playboy Bunny, but—"

"Ah, like one of those Victoria's Secret girls?" He grinned, then switched to a more somber face. "Yeah, I check out that catalog when it comes to the house. You know, to see if there's anything my wife might like for Christmas."

"Right."

"Anyhow, I'd say we got at least a dozen girls in here tonight could fit that description. Excuse me a second." A group of four had entered behind me. He checked their ID, signaled the hostess to seat them, then turned back to me. "So anyway, I'm not sure who's still here and who isn't. Hopefully we're talking about someone over twenty-one."

"Just barely."

"Blond?"

"Redhead."

"Ah, that narrows it down a bit. No curvy redheads that I recall, but you're free to take a look around."

I thanked him and scanned the interior before making my way to the open-air lanai. I'd only met the young woman in question twice—and each time she'd been in the company of five other giggling bridesmaids—so although I remembered her hair color and her stunning figure, I didn't recall much else.

No one in the outdoor crowd even approximated my missing bridesmaid. Most of the people were not in costume, which helped, but not a single woman had the copper-colored hair I sought. She wore it long—I figured it'd cover her back when brushed out. The two times I'd seen her she'd pulled it back into a long ponytail secured by a scrunchie. Of course, on Halloween night she could have been wearing it up, or even under a hat or wig, but besides not seeing the hair, all the gals on the yacht club lanai fell short in the va-va-voom department.

I thanked the bouncer on my way out and joined the swarming crowd on the street. It was slow going, even though the cops had blocked off the full length of Front Street so pedestrians could spill into the roadway. In my tee-shirt and capris I felt pretty lackluster among the scantily-clad naughty witches, greasy-faced clowns and giant talking beer cans.

I stopped in at Cheeseburger in Paradise, as well as half a dozen other bars that were packed so tightly I'm sure the fire marshal was probably home hiding under his bed. It'd be impossible to impose occupancy limits on this night of nights, but it didn't lessen the danger.

After I'd scoured the major Front Street haunts, I decided I'd wait until morning to start seriously asking around. The wedding was still more than a week away—plenty of time for our MIA to show up or contact the bride with apologies for ditching. I turned and retraced the route to my car.

As I passed the second ABC Store in three blocks, I heard my cell phone chiming. I didn't bother to dig it out of my beach bag purse. I wouldn't have been able to hear the caller over the din of the crowd. But even if I could've heard, I didn't want to stop and root through my bag while the heaving throng pushed me in a direction I didn't want to go. I needed to get back to my car. I'd check for phone messages later.

The crowd thinned out at Prison Street with the horde whirling in a giant U-turn back toward the action. I hoofed it up Prison, making my way back to my trashed green Geo Metro. I'd parked it in a spot marked *No Parking—This means you, Brudda!* in front of a yellow shack a few blocks off Front Street. The house looked like it was one smoldering cigarette butt short of an insurance claim; but on the tax rolls the property was probably valued at a million bucks.

I approached the Geo, pleased to see it hadn't been towed or sideswiped by an intoxicated party-goer attempting a three-point turn on the narrow street. But then I noticed something wasn't right. The rear driver's side door was partly open, and in the gritty yellow glow of the sodium street lights I saw a long scratch etched the entire length of the car. Like most locals, I hate Halloween in Lahaina. People use masks and copious amounts of alcohol as excuses to do all kinds of nefarious deeds they'd never consider in day-to-day life. But getting my car keyed wasn't the worst thing that could happen. The gimpy-looking vehicle was an ongoing joke among my friends. I'd already decided that once I pulled together a few more high-caliber weddings like the one I was working on, I'd get myself more respectable wheels.

I opened the rear door, prepared to find a calling card from the joker who'd keyed my car. Maybe an empty liquor bottle or a used condom. Drunken vandals were rarely creative pranksters.

At first I was puzzled by the thing stretched across my back seat, but after a few beats, I figured it out. Then I slammed the door—hard.

A dog began barking a block away.

# 2

Once my adrenaline leveled off, I pulled the door open again. The feeble interior light of the Geo scarcely illuminated the coppery gleam of the long tail of hair. It'd been hacked off just above a black velvet scrunchie. I turned and scanned the shadowy street. Not a soul in sight.

As if it were a dead body, I reached in and lightly touched the hair. It felt warm. It was a balmy night, though, so the fact that it was still warm didn't tell me much. Above the scrunchie, the hair was uneven. It wasn't a smooth cut, like sharp scissors or a barber's razor would have made. It was tangled and messy, as if it had been a hurried effort using a box cutter or a hunting knife.

Although I'm a wedding planner, I'm no stranger to the seamy side of life. I studied criminology in college, using higher education as an opportunity to delve into my fascination with the psychology of evil. After graduating, I trained with Homeland Security and became a TSA Air Marshal at the age of twenty-four. I only lasted ten months in the job, but that was mostly due to my inability to shake off jet lag. On each trip—Honolulu to Taipei and then back again—I'd fall asleep when we were about five hours out. Dozing on the job doesn't make for a stellar performance review, and when I conked out with an undercover supervisor onboard it turned out to be my last free flight courtesy of Uncle Sam. But that was okay with me. I'm a big fan of earth, sea, and sky—in that order. And, I never quite embraced the notion of packing a gun. Since childhood, I've been a serious student of the martial arts. I'm much more confident in my ability to out-punch, outwit, and out-psych my opponent than to place a one-inch slug into the right body part—of the correct individual—while moving five hundred miles an hour six miles up.

I took a hard look at the ponytail before closing the door again. The thick hank lazed languidly across the gray vinyl seat like a skinny fox taking a snooze. All of a sudden I was anxious to get out of there and get home. It hadn't escaped my attention that the hair on my back seat matched that of the missing woman I'd been asking around about. Whoever had chopped off her hair not only had access to a lethal blade, but they'd apparently linked me to her and were keen for me to know it.

The drive back to my house in Hali'imaile took more than an hour—thirty minutes just getting beyond the bumper-to-bumper traffic leaving Lahaina, and then another half hour crossing to the opposite side of the island. Hali'imaile's a few miles up the road from Pa'ia, a funky plantation town on the windward slope of Mt. Haleakala, Maui's highest peak. I like it up there, mostly because it's nowhere near a public beach, and it's miles away from the nearest tourist resort or golf course.

My wedding planning shop—'Let's Get Maui'd'—is officially based in Pa'ia, on the main drag next to a hippie-style grocery store. But earlier that year we'd had a serious fire in the building and the do-gooder historical group that was rehabbing the structure was adamant about allowing only "historically significant" tenants back in once they'd finished. So the hundred-year-old grocery store was welcomed back with open arms, but my wedding shop and the upstairs apartment previously occupied by the store's owner had both been denied occupancy permits. To keep my business afloat, I'd taken up a friend's offer to sublet a dingy space above a four-star restaurant in Lahaina. The shop space was only accessible from the alley. The smell of raw fish every morning was enough to turn anyone vegan, but the rent was dirt cheap. Since moving in, I'd acquired an impressive collection of scented candles, air fresheners, and potpourri in an effort to make it smell less like a fish market and more like an orchid garden. But after eight months I was still pleading my case to the historicals to allow me to come back to my old shop in Pa'ia. In Hawaii, patience and personal connections are highly prized. I had both, and the olfactory challenge I faced every day in Lahaina made me even more determined.

On the long drive home I felt like I was whistling in a graveyard with that hacked-off ponytail following me three feet behind. Once or twice I tried to catch a glimpse of it in my rearview mirror, but I couldn't see it; it was below the reflection. At the stoplight at Ma'alaea Harbor I turned and looked into the backseat, hoping I'd been mistaken. Maybe because I'd been so fixated on the missing bridesmaid's hair color, I'd mistook a rust-colored sweater or a brown feather boa for a coil of hair. I checked. No such luck. It was definitely human hair, and it was still there.

The porch light was on when I pulled into my driveway in Hali'imaile. My roommate, Steve, had gone out partying and there was no way he'd be back this early. Steve's much more than just a roommate, but not in the way you might think. He's a topnotch photographer as well as a superb cook, and he's got a great eye for style. Since his skills dovetail nicely with my profession, I figured it was kismet when he answered my ad offering a room for rent. But we aren't, by any stretch of the imagination, an item. To put it delicately, we both like men. Not that there's anything wrong with that. Only occasionally have we been attracted to the *same* man, and in those rare cases we settled it in a democratic fashion, allowing the object of our desires to cast the deciding vote. Thankfully, so far we haven't run into any undecided voters or hanging chads.

I got out, leaving the hair right where it was, and went in and called my best friend.

"Thank god you're home," I said.

"Hey," said Farrah. "What's up? You sound like you've seen a ghost. Dig it? *Seen a ghost*, on Halloween."

"Very clever. Actually, I'm calling because I've got something I need to show you. Can I come down?"

"No problemo. I turned off the outside lights, but only a few kids bothered to hike it up the stairs anyway. We can pig out on all the leftover Snickers I've got."

Farrah Milton lives secretly above the Gadda da Vida Grocery, the plantation-era grocery store she runs in Pa'ia. Her apartment sustained minor smoke damage in the fire but was left intact, so when the historical society refused her an occupancy permit she stayed with me until after the blessing party for the refurbished store and then quietly moved back into her former digs. She left the *Do Not Enter* signs and the yellow *Caution* tape right where they were and bartered with one of her customers to sneak over at night and replace the blackened and warped treads on the back stairs. Since her store is vital to life in Pa'ia Town no local would dream of ratting her out to the Maui Mo'olelo Society, the politically-connected historical people who now own the land and the building.

I took the stairs two at a time even though it was pitch black in the alley. I'd raised my hand to knock when Farrah pulled the door open. Soft pink light from the living room beckoned me inside.

"Whatcha got?" She looked down at my empty hands.

"It's in the car."

"Too heavy to haul up here?"

"It's *heavy* in the way you'd use the word."

"Whaddaya mean?"

"You'll see."

We clomped down the stairs and I opened the rear door of the Geo and pointed to the dimly lit back seat.

She squinted her eyes. "What *is* that?"

"It's hair."

"Whoa, you're right—that *is* heavy. Looks like the dreads off Rasta Ronald McDonald."

"I think it's the hair of that bridesmaid I told you about. The one nobody's seen or heard from since the bachelorette party last night."

"Bummer. We'd better contact the authorities."

I'd known her long enough to know she wasn't suggesting we dial 9-1-1.

When we got back upstairs, Farrah pulled out a worn deck of tarot cards and laid them on her madras-cloth covered table. She used that same table to eat off of, to groom her hyperactive Jack Russell, and to do covert psychic readings for tourists she solicited in the store below. As she laid out the array, she didn't slap the cards down like a poker dealer; nor did she speak. The cards slipped fluidly from her hands like water flowing over a rock in a stream. With every card she'd nod or widen her eyes but I knew better than to ask questions. She'd speak when she was ready and then it'd come out in a pithy statement that often took me hours to decipher. When she first claimed she had clairvoyant talents I'd scoffed, but time and time again she'd proven her 'third eye' had twenty/twenty vision.

"*Da kine*," she said finally. "Here's what's I see." She passed a hand, palm down, over the line of upturned cards. "What's happening here is strangely cool. I don't think I've ever had this grouping before. You see the Tower card? It signals greed and destruction making way for better things. The High Priestess here symbolizes inner strength and knowing. When these two come forth side-by-side, we're looking at helter-skelter—you know, a clash. Although the Priestess is powerful, the lightning bolt from the Tower seeks to destroy her and she must yield or be doomed."

"In English?"

"There's a ton of weird vibes around that hair. In Hawaiian, we're talking heavy *pilikia*—trouble. I'd say if this hair is from your missing girl, she's in deep doo-doo."

"That's what I was afraid of."

"You know I'm no fan of the establishment, but I think you need to call in The Man on this."

"Should I mention the tarot turned up the Tower and the High Priestess?" I was only half-joking.

"Hey, don't knock it 'til you rock it. Remember, the cops came to *me* to find that dude who tried to swim to Molokai."

"They only called you because his auntie was a mucky-muck assistant to a county councilman and she insisted they try every angle. But I gotta admit, everybody was pretty stunned when you nailed his exact location. *The Maui News* even managed to spelled 'Ouija' right."

"No biggie. Basic CSI."

I squinted.

"Channeling Spirit Images."

I drove back to my house chewing on how I'd file a police report about a severed ponytail showing up on the back seat of my car on Halloween night. I mentally rehearsed the call.

*I'd like to report some minor vandalism. My car got keyed last night in Lahaina. Oh, and while I've got you on the line, somebody left a creepy hank of red hair on the back seat. My psychic friend says it's full of bad juju.*

By the time I got home, I'd decided the police probably had their hands full clearing the streets of the hardcore party animals. It was already past midnight; time to get to bed. I had a nine o'clock meeting with the bridal couple in the morning. Maybe they'd come bearing good news about their friend. Nothing would have made me happier than dumping the severed tresses from my back seat into the garbage and chalking the whole thing up to an ill-advised haircut after too much Halloween hooch.

# 3

Nicole Johnson and Keith Lewis clomped up the stairs to my temporary shop just as I was lighting a third gardenia-scented candle. The garbage truck had been a half-hour late and my shop still reeked of yesterday's catch-of-the-day.

As I welcomed them in, my greeting sounded less than heartfelt, but it was probably just envy. They were both buffed beachy-looking blonds from Southern California, with sprayed-on tans and laser-whitened smiles. They were such a matched set it was kind of creepy—like fraternal twins separated at birth. Besides their good genes, it was hard not to resent their seemingly unlimited money supply. As usual, they showed up wearing yet another pricy gal-guy outfit—a Ralph Lauren mix and match that included front-pleated khaki shorts and deeply-hued polo shirts. His was a vivid jungle green and hers an energetic hibiscus yellow.

"Hey, did you check out Halloween last night?" Keith lifted a fist but I avoided the bump-back by turning toward Nicole at just the right moment.

"Yeah, it was so *amazing*." Nicole stretched the word out to about five syllables.

"They call it the Mardi Gras of the Pacific," I said. "It's rumored to be the largest outdoor Halloween celebration in the world."

"Well, it was f—uh, freaking fantastic." Keith grinned at Nicole. She patted him on the arm and I gathered he'd been making an effort to substitute his favorite f-word for something she found more acceptable.

Although they'd been to my shop once before when we signed the original contract, I noticed Keith's eyes narrowing as he took in the tiny space. The sublet was roughly a fifteen by twelve room with a battered Balinese desk with a chair behind it and two chairs on the opposite side. In the far corner I had a curtained-off area I used for dress fittings. My shop space in Pa'ia was more than twice as big but not, unfortunately, much more elegant. The first time they'd come in I'd explained my current funky digs by briefly describing the fire and the hassle over getting the occupancy permit. But even with my sparse quarters in Pa'ia I prefer a simple workplace. I tell my clients that by spending less on overhead I'm able to offer them more free services than the costly foo-foo wedding planners who have shops resembling Marie Antoinette's boudoir.

"You ready to look at some cakes?"

Nicole gripped Keith's brawny upper arm and leaned into him. "I can't believe we're actually doing this, baby. We've been talking about getting married for so long—and now we're looking at wedding cakes!"

"Yeah, great. Say, do you two girls really need me to hang around? I mean, I like cake as much as the next guy, but the World Poker Challenge Final is on TV right now."

Nicole let go of his arm. Her eyes narrowed; her lips disappeared into a tight line.

"This isn't *my* wedding cake, Keith. It's *our* wedding cake. It's the most major decision we'll ever make as a married couple."

*So*, I thought, *I guess having children, buying a house, living within your budget, and negotiating your sex life fall somewhere short of the cake decision. If so, good luck with that.* But I've learned in delicate situations it's best to keep the smile going and the mouth shut.

"Hey, sweetcakes. I'm here, aren't I?" Keith put his arm around Nicole's waist and pulled her tight against his crotch. "I'll call the hotel and see if they'll DVR the first part of it for me. How long can it take to pick out a cake?"

"Well," I said, "I don't want to drag this out or anything, but traditionally there are two cakes: the bride's cake and the groom's cake. The bride's cake is the big one—usually a multi-layer creation decorated with flowers and fancy icing. The groom's cake is smaller. It's usually done up in a way that has a special meaning to the groom."

"Two different cakes?" Keith winced as if he had a hemor-rhoid acting up. "Great. We'll probably be here all day."

"No, it shouldn't take long," I said. "I've got a nice photo album right here that shows what's available."

I pulled a three-inch binder from my bookshelf. Keith eyed the heavy volume and groaned.

"You're inviting about forty people, right?" I sat down be-hind my desk and gestured for the two of them to sit on the other side. I opened the binder and flipped to the section on mid-size bridal cakes.

"We hope that many will come," said Nicole. "We haven't gotten all the RSVP's back. Can you believe it? We're paying for everything—airfare and all their expenses and still people are too lazy to even send us back the stupid little card. The wed-ding's in ten days. I want to call all the deadbeats up and say, 'Hey people, put the damn little card in the mail or don't you dare show up,' but Keith said that would be rude."

She sniffed and crossed her arms.

I took the moment of silence as an opportunity to nudge her back to the subject at hand. "Well then, let's order a fifty-serving cake. That way, you'll have plenty left over for your first anniversary. And remember, you'll also have the groom's cake. Some people will eat that one instead."

While they flipped through page after laminated page of wedding cake photos, I pondered how to mention finding the hank of hair. I'd hoped they would have expressed some concern over their missing friend without prompting, but since they hadn't, I had to bring it up.

"It's hard to choose, isn't it? Speaking of choosing, I was wondering how you selected your bridesmaids. I mean, six bridesmaids is lot of girls for a small wedding, especially since you're having your ceremony on a boat."

"They're all my best friends forever. How could I possibly decide who to pick and who to leave out?"

"That's true, it'd be hard to choose just two or three. And they're all really pretty girls. I guess it's true what they say about beautiful people sticking together." I was babbling like a beauty pageant contestant answering a tough question, but I was trying my best to maneuver the conversation around to discussing the missing bridesmaid.

"The girls I hang around with are all just like me," Nicole said. "We all belong to the same health club and we all date the same kind of guys—successful ones. We know what guys like in a girl and we dress to impress. Hey, if you don't work at looking good and finding love, you'll end up alone, slaving at some stupid job just to make ends meet." She shot me a pitying look.

I didn't allow my eyes to wander down to my baggy yellow cotton tee-shirt dress and rubber flip-flops—what we call *slippas*. That morning I'd given up trying to find something fetching to wear to this meeting. It'd been months since I'd gone shopping in Honolulu. In fact, the last article of clothing I'd purchased had been a new kung fu uniform. A few weeks earlier my instructor, Sifu Doug, had taken me aside and pointed out my black silk uniform had been washed so many times it had faded to a dusty gray. He said a bad-looking uniform sets a bad example for the younger students, and since I held a black belt they looked up to me as a role model, and so on and so forth. Meeting Sifu Doug's dress code had set me back eighty bucks plus tax.

"Oh, speaking of looking good, have you had any word from...?" I waited for Nicole to supply the name of the missing bridesmaid so I could pretend she'd brought it up first.

"From my parents? No, they're being mean and claiming they don't like to fly. Funny, they don't seem to have a problem flying to Vegas two or three times every year."

"No, I mean, you know, your bridesmaid who didn't come back to the hotel after the bachelorette party on Tuesday night."

"Crystal Wilson? Oh, she's just kind of weird like that. Like you said, I don't need all six girls. And besides, I thought she looked kind of pukey in the super pink bridesmaid dress. She's the totally wrong color for it."

What she referred to as *super pink* is a color most people call *fuchsia*. It looked stunning on her brunette attendants; okay on the blonds. But I had to agree—it looked downright clownish against Crystal's milky-white skin and vibrant red hair. Had Nicole sacked Crystal over a color clash and then covered up her rudeness by claiming Crystal had taken off? That still didn't explain the ponytail on my back seat.

The couple settled on a colossal three-tiered hexagon-shaped lemon pound cake with a vanilla mousse filling studded with fresh papaya. The whole thing would be covered in a bright pink ganache and decorated with handmade white sugar plumerias looping from tier to tier. It was, hands down, the most expensive model in the collection. I couldn't be more thrilled for them, or for my baker up in Kula. She'd probably throw in a dozen free cupcakes for me and Steve.

Then we moved on to the groom's cake. Keith's shoulders sagged as I turned to the tab marked *Groom*.

"Do we have to do this now?" he said. "I mean, I came down here thinking we'd only have to pick one."

I slid the cake book across the desk to him and his face brightened.

"A boob? I can have a boob cake?"

"If you like."

The first cake in the section was an attention-grabbing realistically rendered woman's breast—complete with erect nipple.

Subsequent groom's cakes were done in golf motifs, poker hands, baseball themes and so on, but the breast cake was always the show-stopper.

"Keith, really." Nicole wagged her head as if she felt obliged to feign disdain, but it looked to me like she was more amused than offended.

"Here's the best part," I said, spooling up for the coup d' grace. "If Nicole's willing to provide a photo of her breast, the cake artist can match it. Color, shape, nipple size—everything. But that's if you're okay with that. Otherwise, we'll just go with the standard model."

"Oh, Keith. How cool is that?"

"Way cool. Okay, let's do it. So we're done here, right?"

"Almost. Can you guys come downstairs with me to my car? There's something I need to show you."

"I already missed the poker finale and I'm supposed to play golf at eleven." Keith checked his chunky expensive-looking watch and then gave Nicole a pointed look.

"Yeah, we're kind of in a hurry." She grabbed her purse and popped up from her chair as if she'd just remembered she'd forgotten to turn off the iron in her hotel room.

"I promise this will only take a minute." I'd already made it to the door.

We clomped down the back steps and across the alley to where I'd illegally parked my car in a loading zone.

Keith stopped short. "That's your car? Seriously? Does it run?"

"It runs fine. It's a little *pupuka* from living so near the ocean. You know, salt air is really hard on things."

"Hey, man, don't blame the salt air for that sorry heap. That's the most pathetic set of wheels I've seen since high school. What do they call that color—phlegm green?"

I unlocked the rear door and pointed to the back seat. I hadn't moved the hair from where I'd found it the night before. Even though I'd agreed with Farrah I ought to call the police, I'd stalled off, wanting to see what the bridal couple had to say.

"Any idea what we've got here?" I said.

"Ugh," said Nicole. "What *is* that? It looks like some Hawaiian voodoo thing."

"No, it's a ponytail—with a scrunchie," I said. "And it looks a lot like your friend Crystal's hair, don't you think?"

"I don't think it looks like hers at all. Her hair's lighter. More blond."

I turned and stared at her. She grabbed Keith's hand. "C'mon lover, we've gotta go."

"Nicole," I said, "I found this hair on my back seat last night. I'd been asking around town about Crystal and then when I came back to my car I find this. Pretty odd coincidence, don't you think?"

"Wow, Lahaina was totally crazy last night, don't you think?" said Keith, faking a laugh. "It's probably just a wig from somebody's costume."

"Have you seen or heard from Crystal since the bachelorette party?" I said in a voice I usually reserve for hung-over grooms.

"No," said Nicole in a defiant tone. "But I already told you: she's weird, and she's moody. I'm not worried about her, and you shouldn't be either. She probably hooked up with some guy and they're still partying. Don't stress over it."

"I'm pretty sure this is real human hair," I said. "So, just to be safe, I'm calling the police."

"Uh, I wish you wouldn't do that," said Keith. "I mean, this is our *wedding*. Our friends are coming over here for a good time. If the cops start snooping around, asking a million questions about some chick with a screw loose, it'll wreck the whole vibe."

"Vibe? What kind of vibe do you think I got finding a hacked-off ponytail in my car? And especially since it's the same hair color as your missing friend's."

"Pali, I told you. That's not Crystal's hair," said Nicole. "She's way more blond than that. That's pretty much auburn, and I'd call Crystal a light strawberry blond, right Keith?"

His gaze was fixed at a point far down the alley.

"Keith! I'm talking to you."

"Oh, sorry, what'd you say?"

"I *said*, Crystal's hair isn't that color. It's *way* more blond."

"Yeah. You're right. Anyway, I gotta go. My tee time's in forty minutes and I've got to get down to the driving range for a little practice before then."

"Yeah," said Nicole. "Me too. I've got a pilates class and then at noon the girls are taking me to a fortune teller up in Pa'ia. She's going to give me a tarot card reading. I'm *dying* to hear what she has to say about my future."

There was only one so-called 'fortune teller' in all of Pa'ia who did tarot readings for tourists. I considered calling Farrah to clue her in about who'd be showing up for her twelve o'clock appointment. But then I figured, hey, she's the psychic, she probably already knows.

# 4

I never lock my car. No reason to, and it wouldn't do any good anyway since the lock on the passenger side door's been broken since the day I bought it. I'd never considered it a problem, but after the hair showed up it no longer felt okay to leave my car wide open. I still wasn't worried about car theft—that'd be cause for celebration—but it creeped me out to imagine someone getting in and rummaging around my personal space at will. I wasn't buying Nicole's claim it wasn't her bridesmaid's hair. On TV crime shows, the cops use hair to identify people through DNA testing. I was sure once I filed the missing person report the police would be eager to track down the missing woman. And I'd be able to supply them with Crystal's DNA, because I had her hair—lots of it.

I pulled out my cell phone. It was dead. It'd been doing that lately. It never stayed charged for more than a few hours. I trudged back up the stairs to my shop and plugged it in.

When the phone sparked to life, the message beeper went off. I punched in my code and listened.

"*You have three messages,*" purred the voicemail lady. *Message received Wednesday, at eight-thirty-two.* "Hey, Pali. It's me, Steve. I won't be coming back to the house tonight. Didn't want you to worry. I'll see you tomorrow after work. Have a good one."

*Message received Wednesday, at nine-oh-nine.* From the first word, I recognized Hatch Decker's deep voice. "Hi, babe. It's me. I'm on shift tonight. If you're going down to Lahaina I might see you there. We're taking an extra med unit down just in case. I'm off tomorrow but I'm going out fishing with the guys. I'll be off again on Sunday. Maybe we can hook up then."

*Message received Wednesday, at nine-fifty-nine.* "Hello Pali Moon." The male voice was unfamiliar—even the accent wasn't one I recognized. "I hope you got the present I had them leave for you. Tell Lewis I—" The voice cut off and there was a long pause.

*End of messages.*

I looked up the number for the Maui Police Department. I knew better than to bother nine-one-one with a non-emergency call. "Maui Police Department, how may I direct your call?"

"I need to report a missing person."

"Missing person reports are taken here at our main station in Wailuku from eight a.m. to five p.m. Do you need directions?"

"No, I've been there before."

"Can I assist you further?" In the background, I could hear other phone lines ringing.

"No, *mahalo*, that's all. I'll come in today."

She signed off and I looked at my watch. Still plenty of time to get my errands done and get to the station before they closed.

\*\*\*

Keith and Nicole's wedding was scheduled for Saturday, November 10th onboard the *Maui Happy Returns*—a for-hire catamaran docked in Lahaina Harbor. Hatch Decker, my-more-than- a-friend but not-quite-a-significant-other had given me the name of the boat captain and had vouched he was a reliable sailor. I'd never used this particular catamaran before and I never commit to anything without first checking it out six ways to Sunday, so I headed down to the harbor to inspect the craft and crew.

The day was perfect—the kind of weather the Hawaii Visitor's Bureau plasters on its website and brochures—all golden sun and crystal blue sky with matching sapphire-colored ocean. I had to drive around the harbor area three times before finding a parking spot. I knew I was wasting gas cruising for a spot but something in my local blood won't allow me to pay for parking. The harbor was abuzz with tourists lining up for the early afternoon snorkel cruises to Honoloa Bay and down to Turtle Town. There are a half-dozen spots in South and West Maui that claim the name 'Turtle Town', but that's because the snorkel boat captains simply keep an eye on their fish finders and when they spot a few turtles they drop anchor and announce they've reached Turtle Town.

I walked under the block-wide banyan tree on Front Street, smiling at the kids perched on the limbs waiting for the old man who twists palm frond strips into the shape of grasshoppers. He gives them to the kids for free. My guess is he's either a lonely old guy without any local grandkids or he's an artistic pervert who came up with a good way to hang around little kids all day and not get run off by the cops.

The captain had told me to look for the *Maui Happy Returns* at the furthest moorage on the outskirts of the harbor. I made my way across the splintery wooden dock reading the clever names on the boats and checking out the burgees like the ones I'd seen hanging in the Lahaina Yacht Club. A lot of the boats sported a red flag with a white outline of a whale so I figured that must be the burgee for the LYC.

Crews on the snorkel boats were swabbing down the decks getting ready for the next load of tourists. Everything from rap and reggae to Hawaiian slack guitar blasted from their on-board sound systems. I slowed to watch a well-muscled guy shimmy up a mast wearing only a dark tan, a massive lower-back turtle tattoo, and hip-riding board shorts. Looked like a great way to make a living: plenty of exercise and fresh air; not much paperwork.

At the farthest edge of the harbor I spotted a shiny white hull with plain black letters spelling out *Maui Happy Returns* but there appeared to be no one aboard. I checked my watch. Almost noon. Maybe I'd written the time down wrong.

As I got closer to the boat, I took the opportunity to check it out a bit before getting the official sales job from the captain. In my business first impressions are everything, so if I smelled fish guts or saw a hull encased in green scum I'd be asking for a refund on my deposit rather than a tour.

But all was, as they say, shipshape. Gleaming chrome, polished teak, and well-scrubbed ivory-colored decks signaled a pride of ownership that easily passed my cursory inspection.

"You're early," boomed a voice behind me.

"Not too early I hope." I turned and looked into the face of a guy who fit right in with the tourist bureau's perfect day. He was a bit taller than average, probably two or three inches over six feet, with a well-defined chest outlined behind a damp tee-shirt. His tanned muscular legs—I'm a fool for a good calf muscle—were topped by baggy khaki shorts. I guessed his age at about forty, but his smiling weathered face could have added a few years to my estimate. He wore a white baseball cap advertising the name of his boat. A short thatch of sun-bleached hair poked from under the sides of the cap.

"I hope I haven't kept you waiting long," he said. His smile appeared authentic, and his handshake warm. It was a good thing I already liked his boat. Demanding a refund from a guy that good-looking would've broken my heart.

"No, not at all. Just got here." I nodded toward the catamaran. "Nice boat."

"Very nice. I wish it were mine. I'm Oliver Kingston— friends call me Ono, like the fish. I'm the captain; the owner lives in a Honolulu high-rise."

"Well, he should be pleased with you. It looks like you keep his boat in great condition."

"Not to split hairs, but the owner's a *she*."

Something about the way he said it, it sounded like there was more than an employer/employee relationship between them. I reminded myself my job wasn't to delve into the guy's personal life. I was simply there to check out a wedding venue.

"Well, all the better. May I have a tour?"

"Certainly. Mind removing your *slippas*?"

I've lived in Hawaii all my life, so I already knew to remove my shoes before getting onto a boat—or going in a house—but with my light coloring I'm accustomed to people mistaking me for a mainlander.

"Wow. This cabin will hold, what, thirty or forty people?" I said, looking around the spacious interior. It had a large bar, and padded seats all around the inside walls of the cabin. Big picture windows allowed guests to stay dry if the boat should encounter a rain shower or if big waves kicked up salt spray.

"It's rated for forty-eight, but that'd be a bit tight. But that's just inside the cabin. The entire boat can easily handle sixty-five."

He showed me the bridge where he steered; the heads— what we landlubbers would call restrooms; and then finally the netting stretched like a trampoline across the bow which allowed casually-attired guests to lay back and enjoy the ride while watching the ocean slip by below.

"That's pretty much it. A catamaran is pretty much a *wis-siwig* vessel."

"Wissiwig?"

"Yeah, it's an old software term. It's spelled 'w-y-s-i-w-y-g.' Stands for 'what you see is what you get'. Not many hiding places on an open hull boat like this."

"Well, it looks in perfect shape and I'm sure my clients will be very pleased. You've got us down for one o'clock on Saturday the tenth, right?"

"Yep. I've got a little rendezvous with the owner this Sunday in Honolulu but I should be back by Tuesday. After that, she's all yours for next weekend."

"Could the wedding party have pictures taken onboard before the wedding?"

"No worries. Same day or a day or two earlier?"

"Probably on Saturday morning. That way the bride's hair and makeup will be all ready for the ceremony."

"I don't know how you wedding planner people keep it all straight."

"That's pretty much the whole job—keeping things straight. If you don't mind me asking, how long have you been at this gig?"

"Oh, less than a year," he said. "It's a long story. Say, have you had lunch yet?"

He invited me to help myself to a packaged deli sandwich and a soft drink from the bar refrigerator. As we sat outside on the aft bench, taking in the sun and bobbing in the gentle wake of boats entering and leaving the harbor, I wondered why I'd never considered being a boat bum.

During lunch, I told him about being born in Kauai but raised on Maui. I mentioned my short stint as a TSA air marshal and then told him how I'd fallen into wedding planning after helping a friend with her wedding when her planner bailed on her at the last minute.

Ono followed up by describing his life on the mainland. "I spent the better part of my life laboring under florescent lights. I'd stay up all night wrestling with CAD-CAM drawings and then try to trick my body into thinking I'd slept by drinking way too much coffee. I never questioned my day-to-day existence until my wife, Penny, got cancer."

We locked eyes.

"Yeah, she died. An ugly way to go, no doubt about it." He dropped his head and rubbed a hand across his forehead. "Anyway, I said, 'Screw it' and set off to see the world. As you can see, I didn't get very far."

"I'm sorry."

"Sorry to hear about Penny or sorry I only made it this far?" He smiled, and the sadness lifted a bit.

Finally, I got up to leave.

"You're so lucky to have been born and raised here," he said as we made our way to the gangway.

"Don't I know it."

"Those of us who've come over later in life can't help but wonder what it would have been like to grow up *kama'aina* here on a neighbor island."

"Well, like all things, it's got its upsides and downsides."

"Oh yeah? Give me a downside."

"Nah. It'd sound like whining, and I'm not a whiner. But believe me, there are things you take for granted on the mainland—or even on O'ahu—that we don't have over here."

"Maybe so. But the color came back into my life the day I sailed the *Maui Happy Returns* out of the harbor in Honolulu. I can't imagine where I'd be today if I hadn't met Tomika."

I gave him a puzzled look.

"Tomika Fujioka is my lady-friend in Honolulu. She owns this boat, and she also owns a big piece of my heart."

I nodded. Okay, to tell the truth I was a little disappointed. Hatch and I were doing okay, but there was something compelling about Ono that made me want to get to know him better.

I thanked Ono for lunch and reluctantly disembarked the catamaran. As I crossed the dock, I looked back at the brilliant white hull bobbing in the wake of an incoming boat. I'd never imagined living anywhere other than my little house in Hali'imaile, but at that moment I could've sailed right out of that harbor and never looked back.

***

I checked my watch as I trotted back to my car. It was already after two o'clock and I needed to get the cake order up to Keahou's bakery in Kula. Also, I'd had a call on my shop phone from a prospective client on the West Coast wanting to discuss a Christmas wedding. She said she couldn't talk long since she was calling from work but she wanted me to return her call at around seven her time. It was still daylight savings time over on the mainland, so with the three-hour time difference, I still had an hour to go. I'd charged my cell phone around noon. With the way the battery had been acting up, I'd be cutting it close to have enough juice by then.

I got in my car and glanced in the back, hoping against hope the rightful owner had come by to retrieve her missing locks. No such luck. It was probably my imagination, but it seemed the color had faded a little since I'd first found it. It

looked more bottom-of-the purse penny than shiny-new penny.
Maybe Nicole was right. Maybe I'd leapt to conclusions simply
because red was an unfamiliar hair color in Hawaii. But regardless of whether it was Crystal's hair or not, she was still unac-
counted for.

I had two stops to make before calling it a day: the police
station and Keahou's bakery. Which first? The hair wasn't going
anywhere, and there was no way of knowing how long the cops
would detain me.

Delaying the missing person report was regrettable, but
conducting a wedding without a cake was unthinkable.

# 5

I had the Geo floored as it clawed its way up the steep road to Kula. My agreement with my cake vendor was all wedding cakes had to be ordered—in person—at least ten days in advance to guarantee delivery. I'd stop at the police station in Wailuku on my way back down. The last time I'd dealt with Maui's finest I'd been stuck in an interrogation room for hours. This time I was bringing in evidence, so they'd probably grill me about finding the hair, and then do a CSI number on my car. Who knew how long *that* could take?

Keahou, cake artist extraordinaire, lives in an area we call "upcountry," on the flanks of Haleakala, the island's tallest volcanic mountain. It's always cooler up in Kula. When I was a little kid, I thought the word *cool* came from Kula. It's also very lush. There are farms and ranches and even an upcountry vineyard. With good traffic it takes at least an hour from Lahaina, and since it was mid-afternoon the traffic situation was going from good to iffy as rush hour approached.

"Hey, girl," Keahou said, meeting me at the door with a big hug and a glass of pog—the super-sweet fruit juice every Hawaiian kid guzzles until they graduate to beer.

"Hey, Auntie," I replied. Of course she wasn't my biological aunt. In Hawaii, every friendly female at least a decade older than you is usually greeted as *auntie*, unless they really are related to you in which case they may also be called *mama* or *tutu*.

"You got a cake order for me?" she said. As we went into her house I sucked in the aroma of baking bread, caramelized sugar and chocolate. No doubt heaven smells like Keahou's kitchen.

"Yeah. A big *ono* one." It didn't escape my notice that the word *ono*—which is Hawaiian for *good* or *special*—was also the nickname of a certain boat captain I hadn't quite yet put out of my mind.

"Oh, sounds good. Sit down. Let's see what you got."

I went over Keith and Nicole's cake order and Keahou smiled shyly when I got around to the breast-shaped cake.

"She's going to get you a photo so you can match it."

*"Da kine.* Why all these girls think their boobies so special? Mostly I make the same cake and just make the frosting a little lighter, a little darker, yeah?"

"I agree. You've seen one, you've seen 'em all. But it helps if I offer the personal touch."

"You didn't touch her!" Her eyes bugged out as if I'd dropped my pants.

"No, no. I mean, I tell them to get me a photo and then they think it's a totally customized cake. That's what 'the personal touch' means."

"So 'personal touch' means 'special for you'? I never heard that before. I like it."

"Anyway, here's the written order for both cakes. I need them for the Saturday next, on the tenth. The ceremony's down in Lahaina, on a boat. Then we're going to Gerard's at the Plantation Inn for a fancy dinner and reception. I'll be here by nine in the morning to pick up the cakes."

"This three-tier cake is *pa'akiki*—you know, not easy. And much money. I don't mind carrying it down to Lahaina. I'll get Komo to help me."

"You sure? It's sometimes hard to find a parking place in the middle of town."

"No worries. We know Pako, one of the line cooks down there at Gerard's. He'll let us park in the truck zone for a couple minutes."

I left her with a hefty down payment on the cakes and a pledge to meet her at the Plantation Inn at ten o'clock on the day of the wedding. I knew that for Keahou—and most of the residents on Maui—that meant any time before noon, but I'd adjusted my timetable accordingly.

Leaving Keahou's, I felt my heart rate quicken as I considered my next stop. There's a police station on the West Side—in the Lahaina Civic Center—but I opted for the Wailuku station since it was closer to home for me. Besides, I'd met a couple of the guys there when I'd gotten involved in a crazy proxy wedding last winter, so I hoped I'd run into a friendly face.

Traffic was light on my way down to the Hana Highway and from there I made it to Mahalani Street in less than half an hour. I parked in back and went through the familiar glass doors marked Maui County Police Department. The police station was decorated in classic your-tax-dollars-at-work décor. Everything was beige, with shiny tile floors, low fluorescent-lit ceilings, and a big glass case displaying various awards and citations earned by members of the department and local citizen heroes.

A smiling receptionist sat behind a wide counter on the far side of the room. She wore a wireless telephone headset with a black foam bulb near her mouth. I assumed she was on a call since she was talking in a low voice and there was no one else in sight. Her long black hair was pulled back and as she turned to pull a file from a cabinet behind her I couldn't help but notice the bright blue scrunchie securing her ponytail. I shook off a shudder.

She signed off from her call and turned to me. "*Aloha.* Can I help you?"

"I need to speak to someone about reporting possible criminal activity." I'd rehearsed that line while walking into the station.

"*Possible* criminal activity? What exactly do you mean?"

Okay, so much for my attempt at cop-talk. "I have evidence that indicates a missing girl may have been abducted."

"How old?"

"Well, it was left in my car last night. But this was the first chance I've had to bring it in."

"No, how old is the *girl?*"

I had a strong desire to mutter *never mind* and flee. Were Keith and Nicole right and I was overreacting? "Oh, sorry. She's... I don't know, probably twenty-two, twenty-three years old."

"Then she's an adult female, not a girl." She glanced down as one of the lines on her phone console started to blink. A second later it began humming an almost soothing, *chirr-chirr.* She broke eye contact as she picked up the call. As she questioned the caller, I wondered if maybe she was finished with me. Even though it had been over forty-eight hours, it was starting to look like the police don't consider a missing adult their problem.

I turned to leave. I heard her quietly say, "Hold please."

I was nearly to the door when she said in a much louder voice, "Miss? Please have a seat. I'll have you speak to Detective Wong."

Glen Wong was one of the few guys I'd met at the department. When a crazy wedding I was involved in last winter had gone sour he'd questioned me for what seemed like days, but turned out to be just a little over four hours. Not a hostile guy, but definitely thorough and a bit *aloha*-challenged when it came to dealing with the public.

The receptionist gestured toward a row of beige plastic chairs. "It'll be just a few minutes. He's on the phone."

I hate wasting time. I'd promised to call my potential client on the mainland by four so I pulled out my cell phone.

The receptionist saw me and wagged a finger. "Civilian cell phones aren't allowed in this building."

"Not allowed? Like they're against the law?"

"You're not supposed to use them in here. Only lawyers or sworn officers are allowed to make calls inside the building."

"So, normal people…" I waited for her to answer my implied question.

"We don't get a lot of 'normal' people in here." She smiled as if she'd been waiting forever to use that line. "Civilians need to be at least thirty feet from the building to make or receive calls. But if you leave, I'll have to alert the detective that you're no longer on the premises. His shift's almost over."

Ah, Hawaiian-style bureaucracy. Maybe I'd remember to mention that downside of island life to Ono the next time I see him.

I nodded and took a seat on a chair facing the glass display case. If I'd been in the mood to suck up, I'd have gone over to check out the *attaboy* awards. But by then I was already regretting I'd come in. I'd stick around long enough to file the missing person report and hand over the hair and then at the first opportunity I'd hightail it out of there. My stomach was growling.

Detective Wong appeared a half minute later.

"Hello, Ms. Moon. Good to see you again." He held out his hand and I shook it. Oddly, in my wedding business there's very little hand shaking. Lots of hugs, even some occasional fist-bumps and cheek- or air-kissing, but very little formal hand-shaking. I reminded myself of the handshake protocol I'd learned in federal agent "charm school"—firm, but not gripping; look 'em in the eye; and let go after counting to three.

"Nice to see you, Detective Wong. I'm here with a rather strange situation."

"Okay. Let's find a room and you can tell me all about it."

He led me to a door leading off of the reception area and swiped his ID through the card reader. Once in the hallway, he peeked into the first interior room and found it empty. I was pretty sure it was the same room I'd been in last time, but who could tell? Nothing too memorable about the contents of the room: a metal table with a fake wood-grained top and three metal and plastic chairs. No pictures, no clock, no window except a large framed mirror along one wall which I knew was really one-way glass to an observation area.

"What's up?" He pointed to a chair on the other side of the table and I wondered if that meant we were being taped and he wanted me in good view of the camera.

"Mind if I sit over there?" I nodded to the chair opposite the one he'd indicated.

"Please. Sit anywhere you want. This is your show."

"*Mahalo.* Okay, I don't want to waste your time so I'll get right to it." I launched into a brief summary of the events surrounding Crystal Wilson's disappearance, starting with the bachelorette party; then no one hearing from her the next day; then me asking around Lahaina on Halloween night. The big finale was me finding the hank of hair on my back seat. As I concluded my little speech it occurred to me that the whole thing sounded pretty lame.

"Okay, let's start with names and numbers. Do you have contact information for the friends who first told you this girl was missing?"

I gave him Keith and Nicole's names and told him they were staying up at the Kapalua Ritz. "I've programmed their cell phone numbers on my phone—can I check it?"

"The names and hotel information are enough." His face turned hard, as if allowing me to even peek at my cell phone inside the building would get him in trouble with Internal Affairs or something.

"Do you have the hair with you?"

"Yes, I left it pretty much as I found it. I'm parked in the lot out back."

"I'd like to see what you've got. Give me a minute and I'll catch up with you back in the lobby."

He walked me out to the lobby and then he went through a door on the other side of the reception desk. A few minutes later he came back out and moved a little peg from 'in' to 'out' on a whiteboard with a list of names. Without a word he gestured for me to lead the way and we silently made our way to the parking lot. It would have been nice for him to make an effort at small talk—I mean, I was reporting a missing woman and I was obviously kind of nervous about the whole thing—but he stayed quiet.

As we approached my banged-up car I steeled myself for the usual wise cracks and put-downs but even as the rear door hinge squealed as I pulled it open, he said nothing.

I waited by the door while he leaned in and peered into the back seat.

"This the hair you're talking about?" he said pointing at the ponytail, as if I had a backseat piled with various clumps of disembodied hair.

"Yes, and it's the same color as the woman who's gone missing."

"Huh. And you think this indicates foul play?"

"No one's heard from her for almost two days now."

He stared at the pavement and rubbed a hand across his mouth as if deep in thought. "It's not against the law to cut your hair, you know, Ms. Moon. I guess you could claim this as littering or improper disposal of waste, but I don't really see a crime here."

"There's a woman with hair just like this who's been missing for *two days*, Detective. Oh, and check this out: someone keyed my car when they put the hair in here."

He ran his finger along the deep scratch that ran the full length of the car. "Yeah, I can see that. You're going to need to get that professionally buffed out. It may even require a whole new paint job." He turned and shot me a smile. "If you're looking for a police report to file an insurance claim, just say so. No skin off my nose. But don't sweat the hair. It was Halloween night— in Lahaina. We arrested seven people down there, mostly drunk and disorderly. We caught a couple of guys urinating in public; even had a minor stabbing incident outside the Bubba Gump's. Guy used a dinner fork, can you believe that?"

He stared at me, I stared back.

"Okay, fine. I guess that's it then," I said. I reached for the driver door handle.

"Don't go just yet," he said. "Let me bag this first. You mind hanging out here for another couple of minutes? I need to go inside and grab an evidence bag."

As soon as he was out of sight I looked at my watch. It was already seven-forty-five on the West Coast. I pulled out my cell phone and called my potential client. I got her voicemail.

*Hi! This is Trish. Buddy proposed! If you want to leave congratulations or a fabulous message, wait for the beep. And if you're Susan, get over it. He picked me, not you. Ha, ha! Bye-ee!*

I doubted I could come up with a message on the fly that Trish might consider *fabulous*, so I just left my name and number and then launched into a short commercial message about my shop, 'Let's Get Maui'd.' I told her we were the perfect choice for conducting her nuptials in Maui—*you bring the dream, we bring the team*, yada, yada. I was nearly finished when my phone peeped the low battery warning. I hurriedly ended the call with a sincere-sounding note of congratulations, even though everyone in the world knows you're supposed to congratulate the groom, not the bride. But Trish's voicemail greeting had tipped me off she probably wasn't going to be a stickler for the finer points of wedding etiquette.

Wong returned clutching a wad of evidence-gathering paraphernalia, including a couple of monster-sized plastic baggies, a pair of latex gloves, and a black felt pen. He snapped on the gloves and eased the ponytail off of the seat and into one of the bags. Then he scribbled a few notations on the bag and sealed it up.

"We'll be in touch," he said.

"That's it? Don't you want to write down my statement?"

"I've got what I need, Ms. Moon." He started to walk away, then turned around. "Were you in Lahaina Town last night?"

"Yes, I already told you I was. That's where I found the hair."

"And you were down on Front Street?"

"Yes, I already said that too."

"Drinking?"

"No, I was looking for the missing girl—the bridesmaid."

"It was Halloween, you know."

"Yes, detective, I'm well aware it was Halloween."

"A night for pranks and practical jokes."

"I'm not the joking type, detective."

"No, Ms. Moon, you probably aren't. But if I know anything, it's that all the jokers come out on Halloween. I'll put out a BOLO for your missing young woman, but I'm sure she'll show up on her own in a day or two. Oh, and about the vandalism to your car? I'll get a copy of my report to you within a couple of days. Here's my card if you need the report before then." He handed me his business card and turned and walked away.

I'd assumed I'd feel better once that creepy hair was out of my car. But I didn't. I felt like I'd just shoved Crystal Wilson off a high cliff and I could hear her screaming all the way down.

# 6

I drove to my house using muscle memory. My mind was else-where. Who'd left the hair in my car and why? Was Wong right and it was just someone playing a Halloween prank? More importantly, was Crystal Wilson still missing? I didn't notice the traffic and I didn't remember braking for any stop signs or red lights. I snapped back to the present as I took the right turn from Hali'imaile Road onto my street.

Steve was sitting on the front porch. He waved as I drove around back, and then he met me at the kitchen door.

"I've been waiting for you. Couldn't reach you on your cell."

"Sorry. The thing keeps dying on me." I pulled out my cell phone and showed him the blank screen.

"Well, all hell's been breaking loose here the past couple of hours."

"What's going on?"

"Phone's been ringing off the hook. For starters, Keith, the guy from your La-la Land wedding, phoned at least three times. On the last call he got downright ugly and accused me of not giving you his messages. Farrah's called a couple of times, and then Glen Wong just called a few minutes ago. He wants you to call him back right away. There were a couple others. I wrote 'em down." He pointed to a stack of paper scraps on the counter.

I stared at the stack, plotting my phone-back strategy.

"Hey," Steve went on. "Why's Wong calling you? You find another dead body or something?"

His talk of *another dead body* got me thinking. My reputation as a wedding planner would really take a hit if word got around I was on the grim reaper's speed dial. It'd be wise to keep the ponytail-on-the-backseat and the missing bridesmaid to myself, at least until the police made a move. The last thing I needed was the media getting wind of it and blowing it into a breaking news story about tourist safety going down the tubes on Maui. Steve did freelance photography for *The Maui News* and had a lot of friends in the newsroom, so I played it cool.

"Nah. My car got keyed in Lahaina last night so I went down to the police station to fill out a report. Wong took my statement."

"Ace Detective Glen Wong took a damage report on a car worth about five bucks? My, my, how the mighty have fallen." Steve smiled. He and Wong were good friends and there'd probably be some trash talking down at the gay bar where they both hung out. But Wong was used to keeping secrets—his own and others'—so I was pretty sure he'd keep his mouth shut.

"He was the last guy to leave the station so I guess it fell to him. He's probably calling to tell me he's got the police report ready for me. You know, to file with my insurance claim."

"So, what's going on with Keith? Why's he calling and calling? He got a beef with you?"

"Who knows? I went down to Lahaina Harbor to check out the boat where they're having their ceremony and it's all good. The captain's a nice guy, the boat's gorgeous, and we're all set up for next weekend's ceremony. Say, have you had a chance to talk to them about wedding pictures?"

"Yeah, we talked on Tuesday. They ordered the full meal deal. I'll be shooting nonstop from the minute they get up next Saturday until they're going back to bed that night. I hope they don't want me to stick around for anything beyond that. I'm not into that kind of stuff."

"In more ways than one."

"Funny."

The kitchen phone started ringing. Steve threw up his hands and turned and left through the swinging door.

"Hey," said Farrah. "Why didn't you call me back?"

"My cell died and I just got home. What's up?"

"Guess who I met this afternoon?"

I knew it was Nicole, but friends don't steal friends' thunder. "Who?"

"Your guy—Keith Lewis."

"Really? The guy? Not the bride?"

"Oh yeah, she came in first, but then she wanted me to do him."

"And…"

"You know that creepy ponytail you showed me last night? I got a real strong vibe about that when I laid out Keith's cards. By the way, has your girl shown up yet?"

"Not that I know of. But I took your advice and went to the police."

"What'd they say?"

"Not much. Remember me telling you about Detective Glen Wong from that thing that happened last winter?" Of course she remembered. The "thing" I was referring to had been a personal tragedy for Farrah.

"Yeah." Her voice was hushed, like even the slightest recall of the incident brought it all rushing back.

"He's the guy who took my report. And he took the hair as evidence."

"Well, good. Now you can let it go. It's not your problem anymore. But after reading Keith's cards, I've got a strong feeling he may quickly become a person of interest if your girl stays missing."

"Huh. What'd you see?"

"All I can say is there's some bad juju around those two—especially him."

"He was one cool customer when they came in to order their cakes this morning."

"Go figure. Hey, the guys from the county permit office were over at your shop today."

"They say anything?"

"Not much. A couple of them came in the store at lunchtime to get a sandwich. I did some serious pitching about how small businesses like yours were the soul of Pa'ia Town. They were sympathetic and all, but said their hands are tied by the historical society nut jobs. I think you should consider doing some serious sucking up to Bessie Yokamura."

Bessie was the head of the Maui Mo'olelo Society, and it was pretty much Bessie, and solely Bessie, who determined what was and was not culturally worth saving on the island.

"As soon as this wedding's over I'll think about it. For now, I'm okay where I am."

"That's pretty much how I feel about finding a new place to live. One day they're gonna catch me living up here, but until then, I'm saving a boatload on rent."

We wound up the call, but I promised I'd come by the next morning before heading down to Lahaina.

Next, I called Glen Wong at his office number even though I knew he'd have gone home. The dispatcher asked if it was an emergency or did I want his voicemail. I left a message.

Finally, I called Nicole's cell number. Given the uneasy feeling I had about Keith, I chose to deal with her rather than with him.

"Oh, hi Pali," she said when I announced myself.

"Give me that phone," said Keith in the background. There was a jostling noise and then Keith was on the call. "Where've you been? I've been trying to get hold of you for *hours!*"

"I was checking out the boat for your ceremony. Then I drove up to Kula to order your cakes. I've been working on *your* wedding the entire day."

"That doesn't explain why you don't answer your phone. Maybe me and Nicole wanted to go with you to see the boat."

"My cell phone died. And the reason I didn't invite you to go along is because I needed to check it over first and make sure it was okay. You wouldn't want me wasting your time looking at a scow, would you?"

"Isn't that some kind of pig?"

"That's a *sow.* A *scow* is a boat used to haul garbage."

"Whatever. I need to talk to you—pronto. Can you come over here?"

"Tonight? It's getting kind of late."

Silence served as his answer.

"Okay, no problem," I said. "Give me an hour to grab something to eat, and I'll—"

"No! I've already been waiting forever. Get your ass down here *right now.*"

I quickly changed clothes and grabbed a yogurt from the fridge before heading back out to my car.

Since money obviously wasn't an object in Nicole and Keith's wedding choices, they were staying in a colossal suite at the Kapalua Ritz-Carlton in West Maui. The resort was about as far away as you could get, both symbolically and physically, from my place in Hali'imaile. I took the Honoapi'ilani Highway along the edge of the West Maui Mountains, down to the coast at Launiupoko, past Lahaina Town and then kept going. And going.

The highway necks down at Kapalua and becomes a narrow lane that creeps around the extreme north side of the island like a glorified goat trail. The people who live beyond Kapalua are mostly hardcore locals who don't mind the one-lane stretches and steep drop-offs to the valleys and ocean below. For their trouble, they're rewarded with a pristine natural setting. The constant offshore winds blow across thousands of miles of ocean bringing fresh, oxygen-rich air that's about as unpolluted as any you'll find on Earth.

But I wasn't going that far. The Ritz is situated right before the roadway narrows—the last stop in a long string of oceanfront development that defines West Maui. I pulled into the upper parking lot and made my way past Kumulani Chapel and into the spacious lobby of the hotel. I'd assisted a few brides who'd gotten married at the Ritz—either in the chapel or on D.T. Fleming beach. The on-site staff had always treated me graciously, but I couldn't help feeling like a sticky-faced kid crashing an adults-only party whenever I showed up there. Needless to say, I didn't wear tee-shirts or shorts when I went to the Ritz. For my meeting with Keith I'd gone totally wrinkle-free in polyester black slacks topped by a *faux* silk tunic with Chinese-style bamboo print. Farrah had scored the tunic for me at a yard sale in Wailuku. It looked like it had probably once been part of a bartender's uniform, but the price was right. I'd substituted my ubiquitous *rubba slippas* for a pair of black strappy sandals. In other words, I looked as respectable as I ever got when not attending an actual wedding.

The suites wing was off to my right, but just to be on the safe side, I checked in at the front desk. What with finding the hair, dealing with the cops, and then Farrah's verdict on Keith's creepy vibe, I wanted to leave a clear trail of pebbles should I also go missing.

"Ah, Ms. Moon," said the clerk at the desk. "I have a message for you." He picked up a folded piece of heavy ivory-colored vellum and handed it to me. Inside, Keith had scrawled, *I'll meet you in the lobby.*

I asked the clerk to ring their room to announce my arrival.

About five minutes later, Keith ambled across the marble floor. He'd come alone. His hands were shoved deep in his shorts pockets; his head down. I waited until the last possible moment to rise from the oh-so-comfy upholstered armchair to greet him.

"*Aloha,* Keith. Again, I'm so sorry I was unreachable this afternoon. My phone has decided to go on strike unless I meet its demands for a new battery. And my phone's so old I have to get the battery from off-island—in Honolulu—so it's going to take a while for me to get a new one."

He looked as confused as if I'd spoken to him in Hawaiian—or maybe Greek.

"You okay?" I said, gesturing for him to join me in snagging one of the many unoccupied chairs in the airy lobby. Each of the chair groupings faced the ocean, and from the looks of things, it promised to be a spectacular sunset.

"Can we go somewhere else to talk?" he said, surveying the lobby.

There wasn't another soul in sight except for the two chatting clerks at the check-in desk.

"Sure, but I think we're fine here. I doubt if they've bugged the lobby." I smiled, but Keith's scowl grew deeper.

"I don't want what I've got to say to get back to Nicole. How about we go out to your car?"

"Fine."

As I trudged out of the opulent lobby, I stole a quick backward glimpse of the rose, peach and maroon-streaked sky. What kind of news wouldn't be better received against such a stunning backdrop? Oh well, clients were always demanding things that didn't make much sense to me.

I slipped into the driver seat as Keith wrenched open the passenger door and got in. He sat leaning forward in the seat and stared straight out the windshield. His expression was so grim I half-expected him to pull out a gun and carjack me.

"We gotta talk." He clamped a hand over his mouth as if talking was the last thing he wanted to do.

I waited. He removed his hand.

"Okay, here it is." The words came out in a rush. "I really need you to drop this thing about Crystal. She never was Nicole's friend; she was just some babe Nicole met at her health club who wormed her way into our lives. She was always pushy, always sticking her nose in where it didn't belong. I didn't like her from day one, and Nicole knew it, but she wanted a half- dozen bridesmaids and she wanted a rainbow of pretty girls—you know, blond, brunette, redhead—the whole nine yards. It was hard to find a redhead that met Nicole's high standards so when Crystal showed up, Nicole asked her to be a bridesmaid. Turns out she was a whack job, but even I'll admit she was quite the looker."

"You keep saying 'she was.' Do you know something about Crystal you're not telling me?"

"What do you mean?"

"You keep referring to her in the past tense."

He worked his jaw back and forth a couple of times, then turned to face me. "Look, she's taken off and upset Nicole a week before our wedding. As far as I'm concerned, she *is* past tense and I hope she stays that way."

"What about the ponytail I found on my back seat?"

"Like I said, she's a whack job. She probably cut it off to freak us out and make herself the center of attention. Trust me, right now she's laughing her ass off about the whole thing."

He glanced into the back seat. "By the way, where's the hair?"

"It gave me the creeps so I took it out of my car." I wanted to tell him it was none of his business what I'd done with it, but keeping rude remarks to myself was something I'd been working on ever since I became a wedding planner.

"Okay, here's the deal," he said. "If you'll drop the whole thing, I'll give you a hundred bucks to take that hair off your hands."

"What?"

"That's fair. You won't need to be worry about it anymore and I can toss it and get on with this wedding. I know she's playing us, but Nicole's really freaked out over Crystal taking off like that. I don't want this thing hanging over us."

"Keith, I don't have it anymore."

"Where is it?"

"I gave it to the police when I filed the missing person report."

From the look on his face, I'd say Nicole wasn't the only one who was freaked out.

# 7

I got back home a little after nine. I felt drained, but too wound up to go to bed so early. I stood in front of the open refrigerator hoping to find a forgotten stash of Maui Taco takeout. My stomach growled in impatience so I settled for microwaving some leftover mahi-mahi Steve had grilled the night before.

As I munched on the soggy fish, I sorted through the stack of messages Steve had scribbled on odd scraps of paper: Keith, Glen Wong, Keahou, Farrah, the printer who was doing Keith and Nicole's bridal announcements; and finally, at the bottom of the pile, Ono Kingston. Wait. Steve hadn't mentioned the boat captain had called. Had he called before or after I'd met with him in Lahaina that afternoon? The message was written on the back of a junk mail envelope. I flipped it over. Nothing. Just Ono's name and number.

As much as I tried to deny it, I felt my heart rate pitch up a few notches. My fatigue hopped over to riding shotgun as curiosity slipped into the driver's seat.

If Steve had been home he'd probably have come down to the kitchen by now, but I went upstairs to check anyway. Maybe he was on the phone, or taking a shower, or playing a video game.

No such luck.

It was now almost nine-thirty—a bit late to return calls—so I got to work rationalizing why I needed to call Ono right away rather than wait until morning. He was a new vendor for me. Maybe he had a question, or perhaps he'd run into a snag with the schedule. Or, maybe...*Stop it*, I said to myself—*get a grip.* The guy's got a honey in Honolulu who's not only his love interest but also his boss. Why was I yearning for the mango on somebody else's tree? I had my faults, but playing the 'other woman' wasn't among them.

But that didn't stop me from punching in the number on the scribbled message.

The call went to voicemail. I listened to the no-frills message—*Aloha. You've reached Ono. Leave your name and number*—and caught myself smiling at my reflection in the dark window above the sink. I stuttered a quick message and hung up.

I was emptying the dishwasher when headlights turned into the driveway. I grabbed my purse and smacked on a little lip gloss. Then I recognized the car.

"Hey," Steve said coming through the back door. "You okay? You look kind of weird."

"I'm fine."

"Any news on the hatchet haircut on the disappearing diva?"

"Not really. Keith tried to convince me Crystal's just playing around. He offered me a hundred bucks for the hair. Said it was bumming out Nicole and he wanted me to forget the whole mess."

"Whoa. He wanted you to hand over the hair to him? What'd he say when you told him you gave it to the police?"

"Let's say he didn't look happy."

"And…"

"That's it. He didn't say anything, but he looked a lot more worried than he'd like me to think."

"So what now? You going to drop it?"

"I have no choice. It's in Wong's hands now. Maybe she just took off, like Keith said. But I'm still keeping an eye out."

"Which is business as usual for you. I think working that TSA job made you paranoid. You know, I spent the better part of Tuesday with Ken doll and Bimbo Barbie going over every possible angle of their photo shoot and I'm convinced high crimes and misdeeds are way over their blond-i-locks little heads. I'll bet you ten bucks they think Stephen Hawking sings back-up for Lady Gaga."

"Good point."

Steve bid me goodnight. I rinsed off my fish plate and put it in the dishwasher. Five minutes later, I was in bed.

***

At seven the next morning I drove down to Pa'ia. I pulled into the alley behind my former shop space which shares a common wall with Farrah's grocery store. The back door to the shop was open and I heard male voices inside. No work sounds, just loud voices and laughing. I went inside and all conversation ceased.

"Hey, Pali," said Tiko, one of the building inspectors from the county office. I'd met him right after the fire, when he'd annoyed me by nailing a 'No Trespassing' sign right into the mahogany of my front door.

"Hey, Tiko. What bad news you got for me today?"

"Not so much bad news, just *hoihoi*—interesting stuff." He turned to the two other guys standing in what had been the office area of 'Let's Get Maui'd'.

"Yeah," said one of the guys. "We heard you got new digs down in Lahaina."

"Just temporary. I'm waiting to move back up here once the Mo'olelo Society gives me the go-ahead."

"Oh well then, sorry, but maybe it is bad news. Looks like you moving back's not gonna happen."

I turned to Tiko.

"Yeah," he said. "I'm here to write up an occupancy permit, but it's not for your wedding store."

"Are you going to make me do twenty questions, or will you at least give me the respect of spilling who *cock-a-roached* me out of my shop space?"

"Pali," he said, pointing to the two men standing next to him, "these guys are from the Maui Mo'olelo Society. This is Bono and that's Mike."

They nodded.

"So, the Mo'olelo Society's finally getting around to blessing a tenant," I said. "But it sounds like it's not me."

"'Fraid not," said Tiko.

"So? Who is it?"

"It's them."

It took me a second to figure out what he was saying. "The Mo'olelo Society wants to move in here?'

"Yep. It's their building now, and they're about as historical as it gets. They're going to turn it into a visitor's center."

"But it's too small. Look around, it's only about five hundred square feet. Way too cramped for a visitor center."

Bono spoke up. "We always wanted a little outpost in Pa'ia, but we couldn't afford the rent. When they had the blessing party for this building Bessie looked around and said she thought this would be perfect. We don't need much. Just a desk and some brochure racks."

It made sense, but I hated the idea of being shoved out. As he'd said, it was nearly impossible to find affordable shop space in Pa'ia.

"I'm going fight this. You can't just come in here and throw me out. I paid my rent; I was a model tenant for two years."

"A model tenant in an historic building. Sorry, but that's progress—or I guess I should say, anti-progress," said Bono. "I doubt you'll get much support if you fight us. The merchants up and down this street will love the idea of tourists stopping in here rather than just blowing by on their way to up to Hana."

Pa'ia was on the famous road to Hana, a must-do tourist attraction. Unfortunately, most tourists didn't stop in Pa'ia except maybe to buy a quick sandwich to sustain them on the three to four-hour drive.

I went out back to wait to go up to Farrah's apartment. The Mo'olelo guys were probably well aware she was still living up there, but everyone acted as if it were a well-guarded secret. When I saw their car moseying down Baldwin I went up and rapped on the door, using our little code knock. She opened up so quickly I assumed she'd been standing on the other side also waiting for them to leave.

"How's it going?" I said.

"Can't bitch, and too old to moan." She motioned for me to sit down in my usual spot. "You want coffee?"

"*Mahalo*. Say, did you hear who your new neighbor's going to be?"

She shot me a sympathetic look and nodded.

"What am I going to do? I can't take that fishy smell much longer, and it's killing my business to ask clients to come through a back alley and clomp up those rickety stairs to spend twenty thousand bucks on a wedding."

"You want me to work a little black magic?"

"No, but keep your ears open, okay? I've got to find a place for my shop."

She served the coffee and we settled in our usual spots—me in a ratty orange director's chair and Farrah on her forlorn-looking velveteen sofa.

"Guess what our pal Keith did last night?" I said.

"Confess to some heinous crime?"

"Hardly. He made me drive all the way to the Ritz and then he tried to give me a hundred bucks to forget I'd ever seen that hair."

"What's that about?"

"He says it's upsetting Nicole and he wants us all to move on and consider Crystal's disappearance simply her pathetic attempt to grab the limelight away from Nicole."

"Why'd he offer you money? Why didn't he just ask you to give him the hair?"

"Keith strikes me as the kind of guy who thinks everything has a price."

"Funny you mention it. He handed me a hundred dollar bill for a thirty buck session, then told me to keep the change. That was even before I got started. It felt like a bribe."

"He's loaded. I hope you kept it."

"Would you have taken his money for the hair?"

"No way."

"Well, me neither," she said. "I told him to tip his hotel maid. Those girls work hard and get paid slave wages. Besides, I don't like the feeling of being bought off."

I knew what she meant. There's a weird push/pull in living and working in a tourist destination. We all need a lot of money to live in Hawaii's inflated economy, but most of us resent the step-and-fetch-it relationship it creates with the visitors we serve.

"Anyway," I said. "You got any details for me on Keith's visit yesterday?"

"I don't know. I probably should keep my mouth shut."

"Why?" I said. "Did he say something bad about me? Or is it that you think I'll freak out over something you'll say?"

"All I can say is that guy puts a capital 'C' on the word 'creepy'. Where'd you snag those two, anyway?"

"Internet. They told me they loved the gorgeous website Hatch whipped up for me while he was down for the count." Firefighter Hatch Decker had spent most of February on my sofa recuperating from a broken leg. He'd jumped at the opportunity to work on a project he could do while sitting down.

"Well, maybe he needs to update that website with a 'no creeps allowed' sign. You know, a circle with a creep in it and a red slash across?"

I tried to imagine what the symbol for 'creep' might look like, but she'd already moved on.

"First I did his basic astrology chart. It turned out really strange. And then I laid out his cards. He gave off a totally bizarre vibe and asked the weirdest questions. I'd already done Nicole, and there wasn't much there. She's got a pale yellow aura, and she had pretty typical cards. Keith's aura started off blood red, then turned dark—almost black. Look, I'm getting chicken skin just thinking about it." She leaned over and showed me her forearm.

"You think they're incompatible?" I said.

"Can't say. But I found myself blabbing all kinds of fluff to her like 'Loyalty may be less valued by your loved ones than you'd prefer' rather than coming right out and saying, 'This guy's an *apuka* and he'll cheat on you every chance he gets.' It wasn't so much incompatibility I was seeing, as it was deception."

I rolled that around in my mind. "Maybe Keith was just messing with you—you know, to try and throw you off. See if you were for real."

"Could be. I get lied to a lot. But auras don't lie, and that guy's was freakazoid. But, hey, I'm telling you too much. My sessions are supposed to be confidential."

"Well, if it helps, I'll let you in on a secret of my own. I'll keep yours, you keep mine."

At that point, there was a rap on the back door of the grocery store downstairs and Farrah got up to peek out the window.

"Egg man's here," she said. She went downstairs to let him in and I followed. The egg man brought in a few dozen organic brown eggs from his little chicken farm up in Makawao every other day. Farrah paid him out of her cash drawer, and he disappeared as quickly as he'd shown up.

"Sorry about the interruption."

"No worries. Anyway, here's my *hush-hush*—I met a great guy yesterday."

She widened her eyes. "You mean a boyfriend-type guy? What about Hatch? I thought you two were an item."

"Hatch and I are, well, friends. It's like this—he's got today off but instead of hanging out with me he's going fishing with his buddies. So, whatever our relationship is, it's not that serious and it's definitely not exclusive."

"I don't know. Sounded pretty serious when I called your house and you were making him breakfast."

"Okay, then I'll cop to us being friends with benefits. But that weekend you called was almost a month ago. Anyway, the new guy's name is Ono Kingston. He's the captain of the catamaran we're taking out for Keith and Nicole's wedding."

"Yeah, speaking of that—it kind of steamed me they didn't want me to perform their wedding ceremony. I'll bet your 'Captain Ono' doesn't even have a nice spiritual script like mine."

"Or a lavender caftan." I imagined Farrah in her billowing wedding garb. With her frizzy waist-length hair and ample bosom, she looked like a forest fairy on steroids. "Well, don't stress over it. I don't think those two or their forty friends will be listening to the ceremony much anyway. With them it's all about the photo op and the party afterward."

"Yeah, well. So, tell me more about this Ono guy."

"Okay, but I don't have that much to tell. He's from the mainland. His wife died of cancer and he came over here to get over it. He seems like a really nice guy."

"And he owns a big-ass fancy boat," said Farrah.

"Actually, no. He's the captain. It's owned by someone in Honolulu."

"Okay, remember me—your psychic pal? It doesn't take a psychic to know when you hedge around and say 'someone' you actually mean 'a woman.' So, what's with that?"

I shrugged.

"He's skippering his girlfriend's boat? It's not like you to be checking out guys who are already taken. Kind of goes counter to being in the wedding business, don't you think?"

"You're the one who's always nagging me that I live like a nun. I thought you'd congratulate me on actually noticing a good-looking guy."

"Yeah well, it sounds to me like he's already been noticed. So cut your line and throw 'em back."

Farrah and I stood there, staring each other down until the phone on the back wall started ringing. Farrah waved it off, but it kept on—five, six, seven, rings.

"Okay, okay," she said as she made her way back to pick it up. "Probably some tourist wants to know if I carry the LA Times. I love to say 'yeah sure' and then listen to the dead air when I tell 'em it's always yesterday's edition."

She picked up the receiver. "*Aloha*, Gadda da Vida Grocery." She stared at the ceiling as she listened. "Uh-huh. Yeah. Hang on." She handed me the handset. "It's your live-in honey buns."

"I'm glad I found you," said Steve. "Glen Wong's up here and he says he's not leaving until he talks to you."

"Okay, put him on."

"He wants to see you in person. He's been here a while. When are you coming home?"

"I'm sure you've been enjoying playing the charming host to Detective Wong." I winked at Farrah. I was treading on shaky ground since Steve had told me in strictest confidence he'd had a little crush on Glen Wong ever since they'd first met.

My indiscretion was greeted with an echoing silence.

"Okay, sorry. Tell Wong I'll be up there in ten minutes." I considered making another teasing remark, then let it go. I needed Steve to do the photo shoot for Nicole and Keith, and besides, he'd never once blabbed about my many embarrassing foibles. Anyway, not any that I'm aware of.

I hung up and turned to Farrah.

"Sounds like you've gotta go," she said. "But before you leave, tell me what the police said when you filed the missing person report."

I briefly described my trip to the police station and how Wong had shrugged Crystal's disappearance off as a prank.

"And now Wong's up at your house? Maybe he's changed his mind." She opened her cash drawer and started sorting the coins in the till. "If you need back-up for your story, I'd be happy to give him the four-one-one on that dude's creepy aura."

"*Mahalo.* I'll let you know how it goes."

As I turned right on Hali'imaile Road I saw a Maui Police Department blue and white Crown Vic parked on the street in front of my house. I could feel the beady eyes of my neighbors hidden behind drawn drapes or lowered bamboo shades. No doubt they'd been keeping a constant vigil ever since the police car pulled up.

I parked in back and went in through the kitchen door as usual. I heard Glen Wong and Steve in the living room. They were laughing. No loud guffaws or snorts, just the kind of polite laugh people do when they're talking story while cooling their heels, waiting.

"Honey, I'm home," I sang as I pushed through the swinging door separating the kitchen from the living room.

Steve shot me a doleful look. I'd really worn the edge off that greeting, and he seemed especially mortified I didn't have the good sense to stifle myself when we had official company.

"So you are," he said. "But it's been way more than ten minutes."

I considered throwing him a *shaka* sign with the 'Maui time' excuse, but figured he'd had my back on this one. No use pushing my luck.

"Sorry, I got held up at Farrah's store."

Glen frowned. 'Held up' probably isn't the best phrase to use to tell a cop you've been detained. He rose to greet me, extending his hand. I shook it and he sat back down on the sofa. I took the chair opposite.

"Ms. Moon, I felt it necessary to come by and let you know how we're proceeding with the report you filed yesterday."

Steve took the cue. "You guys want anything to drink?"

In unison, Wong and I said, *mahalo,* but no.

"Well, I've got some paperwork to catch up on. I'll see you guys later." He nodded to Wong and then took the stairs up to his bedroom on the second floor.

Wong leaned in toward me. I expected him to start firing questions, but he remained silent.

I waited.

He cleared his throat. If I didn't know better, I might have taken the guy for shy. It seemed he was working his way around to saying something embarrassing.

Finally he spoke. "I reviewed this with my chief and we're in agreement that this is most probably a hoax. Simply a Halloween prank."

"You think a severed ponytail from a woman who's been missing for two days is simply a prank?"

"Well, the hair you brought in has yet to be positively identified as to ownership, and when we called the names you gave me as the woman's friends they gave a logical explanation for her whereabouts. But I need to complete my report to close the file. You know, whenever a citizen contacts us we need to investigate. Can't just ignore it."

Seemed to me that was exactly what he was doing, but I kept my mouth shut.

He pulled a little notebook out of his shirt pocket and flipped through the pages before settling on the one he wanted.

"The hair was cut, not pulled from the scalp, so most likely the person wasn't harmed. Also, because we have no follicle from the hair it's unlikely we'd be able to find much DNA. But we wouldn't order such a test anyway, because it's expensive and time-consuming and we have no reason to suspect a chargeable crime here."

He stopped and looked over at me as if expecting a rebuttal. I stayed silent.

"Anyway, the people you named as acquaintances of the woman, a Keith Lewis and a Nicole Johnson, who are staying up at the Kapalua Ritz, both gave plausible reasons for the woman deciding she no longer wanted to be in the wedding party. Ms. Johnson said the woman expressed some reservations about wearing the bridesmaid dress. Wrong color or something."

He shot me a half-smile.

"She's missing," I said, not giving him any time to start up again. "No one's seen her in three days now, and she's contacted no one. Doesn't that cause you any concern?"

"Not really. As you know, Ms. Moon, visitors come and go with every plane in and out of Kahului."

"I know that," I said. "But have you checked with the airlines to see if Crystal Wilson was aboard any of those outbound flights?"

"If I thought there was any reason to check, I'd do it. But so far I'm not convinced there's a problem. We appreciate your concern, but we think it's unfounded. *Mahalo* for your time." He snapped his notebook closed. "If you hear anything you think I ought to know, please feel free to get in touch." He handed me yet another of his plain black and white business cards.

"Okay, I think you ought to know I'm pretty stunned you're taking this so lightly. I've got a really bad feeling something horrible has happened to this girl. When her family and friends from the mainland start calling and asking questions, I'll bet you'll be hard-pressed to wave them off as easily."

"You're entitled to your opinion, Ms. Moon. But I don't think that's going to happen. You seem to revel in imagining various intrigues involving visitors. But this one's a non-starter. I'm advising you to heed the request of your wedding clients and let this thing go. Get back to fussing over dresses and flowers and leave the investigating to us." He stood. "Now, if you'll excuse me, I need to get going. I'll let myself out."

He quietly pulled the front door closed behind him. I started counting. Sure enough, I'd only gotten to eight when Steve bounded down the stairs.

"He left so soon. Is everything okay?"

I shook my head *no* but didn't say anything.

Steve crossed the room and pulled the bamboo window shade aside a few inches. He peered down the street.

Finally I spoke. "Your pal Glen Wong thinks I'm paranoid, or a meddler, or maybe both. In any case, he advised me the police aren't going to be looking into Crystal Wilson's disappearance—now or ever."

"Really? I'm surprised. He seemed pretty agitated when he first showed up."

"Probably just the pitter-patter of his heart when he saw you were here all alone."

"Don't start."

"Okay, sorry. I'm just kind of stunned he blew me off like that. He hasn't asked around at all. He's completely convinced it was just a Halloween prank."

"And you think he's wrong?" He let the shade drop and turned to face me.

"Of course I think he's wrong. I know something bad happened to that girl. And I believe whoever left that hair in my car is one dangerous guy."

"Or gal," he said.

I squinted at him.

He lifted his chin. "Hey, Ms. 'Politically Correct' Moon— crime's an equal opportunity employer, wouldn't you say?"

# 8

I was boring Steve by rattling off everything I could remember about the two times I'd seen Crystal Wilson when the phone rang.

"I'll get it," he said. He banged through the swinging door to the kitchen, leaving me wondering if maybe Wong was right and I was simply seeing bogeymen around every corner. There was no denying fuchsia was an ugly color on a redhead like Crystal.

A few seconds later Steve pushed the door open about six-inches and said, "It's for you."

"Is it a guy?"

"I think," he said in a low voice. "But that Samoan woman who bakes your wedding cakes has a voice like a guy so I can't be sure."

When I picked up the phone, a deep rumbling voice said, "*Aloha*, Pali." It was definitely not Keahou up in Kula.

"Oh hi, Ono. How're you doing?"

We went through the usual pleasantries for half-a-minute before he got down to business. "I have a favor to ask."

"Okay, shoot." I thought that sounded a little tough, so I attempted to crank up the femininity a tad. "I'd be happy to help in any way I can."

"Great. Here's my problem: I'm headed over to Honolulu this weekend to do a sailing party for the owner and my cabin girl is sick. Well, not actually sick, she got a nasty infection from a dirty needle at a tat shop. Her back's so puffed up she looks like a beached turtle."

I didn't say anything. Not that I didn't feel bad for the poor girl, but I was contemplating what I suspected was coming.

"Anyway," he went on, "I need a hostess to help serve drinks and food at the party. My first mate can mix drinks and help me at the dock, but I need a pretty face to make sure everyone has a good time."

Again, I was silent. The *pretty face* comment was working its way through my BS detector.

"We'll only be gone a couple of days. Well, actually, three. We'll go over early tomorrow, then stay Sunday for the party, and then we'll head back at oh-dark-thirty on Monday morning. I know you've got this big wedding coming up, so if it's too much to ask, just say so. But you seemed so cheerful when you came out to the dock yesterday I thought you might get a kick out of it. Oh, and it pays a couple hundred bucks—not that you probably need the money—but just in case you were wondering."

Ha! Little did he know how much I'd welcome an unexpected two hundred dollars.

"You're not saying anything," he said. "Have I insulted you? Am I way out of line here?"

"No, not at all. It's just that I'll need to check my calendar. Can you give me an hour or so and I'll call you back?"

"Of course. No worries. I just thought you might enjoy it. I stay at the owner's high rise when I'm over there and she's the consummate hostess. First class all the way. The first mate's got some old high school buddies he hangs out with, but Tomika always insists I stay with her."

*Lucky for you,* I thought, *but I'll be hard pressed to find a last-minute hotel room in Honolulu that won't cost me most of the two hundred bucks.*

"Well, it sounds like fun," I said. "Can I get back to you by noon?"

I hung up the phone wondering why I hadn't simply declined right away. Was I some kind of masochist? Maybe I was way nosier than I admitted. Or was it that slipping out to sea, sailing past Molokai, and over to O'ahu with a gorgeous boat captain at my elbow and the wind in my hair made me think of that *king of the world* thing?

Spending three days with charming Ono, even though it meant coming face-to-face with his love interest, was probably worth it. And besides, meeting his wealthy, sophisticated girlfriend would most assuredly snap me out of my reverie and make me focus on the task at hand: figuring out where I stood with fireman Hatch Decker.

***

I made the rest of my callbacks and soon it was almost noon. I went through my to-do list for Keith and Nicole's wedding and found only one item that still required my attention—selecting the limo cars and drivers. I'd heard that on the mainland wedding planners simply sign up with a reputable limo company and they're assured of clean, well-appointed cars that arrive at the right place at the right time. The cars would be gleaming, inside and out, and the drivers would be in freshly-pressed uniforms. Moreover, they'd be gracious and accommodating—knowing such behavior would earn them a good tip.

On Maui, it wasn't that simple. I'd once used a limo company that had given me good cars and drivers for months and then—without warning—disaster. Later, I found out the owner had grown tired of the business and had handed it over to his teen-aged nephew as a high school graduation gift. The next time I used them, clueless nephew showed up half-an-hour late wearing a tee-shirt splattered with plate lunch. Then, he tried to bum twenty bucks off my client for gas. He had the radio blaring rap songs with lyrics that would have been bleeped out on TV. The limo interior was littered with beer bottles, fast-food wrappers and a girlie magazine. When my enraged client called me on his cell phone, I contacted the limo service to demand another car and driver. They said 'Take it or leave it' as it was prom night at Lahainaluna High School and every car for hire on Maui was already spoken for.

Now I personally inspect all limos and interview the drivers the week before the wedding. It only takes about an hour, so I figured I'd schedule it for Tuesday—Wednesday at the latest.

I called Ono at five to twelve. "I'm in. Tell me what I need to do."

\*\*\*

It's odd that I've lived my entire life surrounded by water but I rarely go near the water. For me, the ocean is like the sky—it's just there. When I was an air marshal and we'd take off from Honolulu and spend hours upon hours streaking over the flat, blue-black Pacific I thought of it as merely space and time. It wasn't wet, or cold, or alive with creatures, it was simply something to cross—a wide gap between Point A and Point B.

Standing on the deck of the *Maui Happy Returns* as it slid out of Lahaina Harbor at five a.m. on Saturday morning was an experience I won't soon forget. The motion of the boat felt odd, as if I was half-asleep and my perception was slipping in and out of reality. The trade winds were blowing pretty strong, and as we cleared the harbor area, Ono motioned to Chico, the first mate, to raise the sail.

Chico hopped up on the roof of the cabin and cranked the winch on the main mast, releasing a huge expanse of white sail. It fluttered and caught the wind like a colossal cupped hand, and before long we were flashing across the waves, slipping down into choppy troughs and popping back up at a dizzying speed.

I stood near the back of the boat, one hand shielding my eyes from the rising sun and the other hand gripping the rail. Watching the glowing white sail bulge and then relax against the wind was hypnotic.

"Pretty nice, huh?" Ono yelled to me from his place at the stern.

"Fantastic," I said. I went up the four stairs to stand by him at the wheel.

"You get out on the water much?"

"Never."

"Yeah, it seems like that to me too, sometimes. I can never get enough."

"No, I mean, I can't remember the last time I was out on a boat, or even in the water. Maybe back in high school."

He touched my shoulder and I turned. His face looked stricken, like I'd told him my dog just died.

"Honest? You live here on Maui and you never go out? I took you for a long boarder or maybe a windsurfer."

I laughed. "Nope. I'm pretty much a land-based life form."

"Well, you're doing great. This isn't the easiest crossing. We've got pretty solid seas today but it can really slam you around if you don't watch the weather. We'll be in the lee of Molokai here in a bit. Until then, you'd probably be better off down in the cabin."

I went back down the steps, gripping the handrail as the catamaran charged up a ten-foot swell. By then, Chico had jumped down from tending the sail and was busy getting soft drinks out of the refrigerator. He handed me a cold can.

"*Mahalo.*" I'd been so busy getting my sea legs I hadn't really observed Chico. His arms were heavily tattooed from shoulder to wrist. A thick green sea serpent wrapped around his left ankle and up his calf ending in a fierce-looking dragon's head above his knee. Chico was barefoot, with khaki shorts and a white cotton strap-shirt completing the ensemble. No doubt there was more ink on his chest and back, but I couldn't see through the shirt.

"What's with the tattoos?" I said. "It seems everybody I know is sporting some kind of body art."

He smiled and nodded. "It's a sailor thing. All us sailors do it."

"Yeah, but it's not just sailors. Everywhere I look it's something—an ankle charm, a tramp stamp, whatever. Every high school girl on the island has some kind of goofy tat—a sea horse or a flower. I heard your cabin girl's sick from getting a dirty tattoo. So what's with all the ink?"

"It's cool. Makes you special. Like this," he pointed to a dolphin leaping out of a wave on his brawny bicep. "This is for my dad, ya know? He loved dolphins. When he died, I had this put on me to remember him by."

"You wouldn't remember your father otherwise?"

He grinned.

Ono waved for Chico to take the wheel.

"Gotta go," said Chico. "You better hang on, it's gonna get kinda rough for awhile."

After an hour about a dozen dolphins showed up. They surrounded our boat in a churning mass, racing alongside so close to the front of the hull I thought we'd mow them down.

"How do they do that?" I said. "They seem to know which way we're turning, which is a good thing or they'd bash into the boat or get run over. You ever see them get hurt?"

"Trust me," said Ono. "These guys are way smarter than we are. They swim all day, just looking cute for the tourists and munching on little fish. You don't see them slumped in front of a computer screen or nailing roof tiles in the blazing sun. Maintaining a safe course is pretty much their only concern."

At the mention of the word *concern*, Crystal's disappearance flashed into my mind. I wasn't buying Wong's Halloween prank theory, and Keith and Nicole's indifference—coupled with the memory of her hair lying across my back seat—had me spooked. The further we got from Maui, the more I became convinced I should do something. But what?

For five more hours we zipped across the water; the waves slapping the hull, then sending a blast of sea spray onto the deck. I spent most of the time outside gripping the rail, but at lunchtime I made my way down into the cabin and pulled a sack of sandwiches out of the refrigerator to offer the guys.

Ono was back at the wheel and Chico was alongside the mast, tightening a winch. "Hey, Chico," said Ono, "when you get done there, would you mind checking how we're doing for booze and mixers? We may need to go shopping in town."

Chico jumped down and banged through the cabin cupboards, counting bottles.

"We're low on gin and we could use a gallon of guava juice for the mai tais. But besides that, it looks pretty good."

"So, speaking of booze," I asked Ono when I handed him his sandwich, "will I be mixing drinks? I'm kind of rusty. I worked as a waitress a few years ago, but mostly it was just serving. My manager claimed the bar lost money whenever they let me pour."

"No worries. Chico's the bartender. You just have to see that everyone's having a good time and make sure the food platters are full. You'll be Tomika's 'girl Friday.' Your main job is to make her look good and make sure the party goes off without a hitch."

"Right up my alley."

\*\*\*

At about four-thirty I could see the island of O'ahu dead ahead. The bumpy part of the ride was behind us as the water changed from fierce chop to smaller rolling waves.

"See that point over there?" Ono pointed out a spit of land, topped with a steep cliff. "That's our heading. Just beyond it, we'll tack north-northeast and slip right into Ala Wai Harbor. Should be docking there in just over an hour."

My hands clenched. I didn't want the ride to be over; or maybe it was that I was nervous about meeting Tomika. Whatever it was, I had to take a few deep breaths and talk myself down from feeling panicky.

We pulled into Ala Wai Harbor and I was shocked by the condition of the water. Garbage and litter floated freely among the boats and there was a wide ribbon of oil sheen twisting in and out of the moored boats.

"Ick, this place is filthy," I said.

"Yeah, they've been vowing to clean up Ala Wai Harbor for years now. They make an effort in starts and fits, but it just never seems to get done. It's fed by the Ala Wai Canal, which goes through town, picking up wastewater and garbage—even though it's illegal to dump stuff in the canal—and by the time the water gets here it's pretty foul. Also, there are a lot more vessels in and out of here than in Lahaina, so the harbor gets dirty from all the coming and going."

We motored into a mooring marked 'Honolulu Yacht Club' and Chico jumped out and tied us up.

"How does this work?" I said. "Do we have permission to dock here?"

"Sure do. This is Tomika's slip. She pays a fortune to lease both this one and the one in Lahaina. But don't worry about her, you can bet she's not missing any meals to pay her moorage fees." He winked at me, and I had the prickly feeling I was colluding with a gigolo.

"Well, lucky her. What should we do to get ready for tomorrow's party?"

"You mean right now?"

I nodded.

"Nothing. Chico will run to the liquor store and get the stuff we need, and the caterers will come aboard about an hour before we sail tomorrow night. You're pretty much off the clock until then."

"Okay, good. One more question: how do I get into town from here? Do busses come down this way?"

He looked puzzled. "I suppose they do. But Tomika will send her driver. You don't need to worry about getting around town."

I went below deck and picked up my overnight bag. I'd packed light—a couple changes of underwear, a Hawaiian-print sundress to wear at the party, and my make-up. My idea of full-blown make-up is mascara, blush and lip gloss. Just like the catamaran, I'm pretty much 'what you see is what you get.'

We slipped on our sandals and hopped onto the dock. Ono pulled a few bills out of his wallet and handed them to Chico.

"Be back here by four tomorrow. If I don't see your *pupuka* face by four fifteen, you'll find yourself swimming back to Maui," he said with a grin.

"Don't worry, man, I never been late on you yet."

We walked out of the harbor and when we finally reached the street I was hit by the wall of noise that characterizes Honolulu. 'Honolulu' means 'sheltered harbor' but I think it should mean 'tall and loud' because that's what it is. I gazed at a forest of soaring skyscrapers that seemed to have doubled since I was in college here only eight years ago. In Manoa, the neighborhood where the University of Hawaii is located, it's still pretty much low-rise. But Ono and I were on Ala Moana Boulevard, looking right into the heart of the bustling city. I felt like a country hick in my wrinkled khaki shorts and tee-shirt.

"Any ideas on where I should go tonight?" I said.

"You want to go out? Like to a show or something?"

"No, I'm planning on turning in early. Today was way more fresh air and excitement than I'm used to. I need to find a reasonably-priced hotel."

Ono stopped and turned to face me. "You're not staying at Tomika's? She's looking forward to meeting you."

Okay, this was getting awkward.

"I didn't know I was invited," I said. "I thought you and Tomika might want to be alone."

"Hell no, we see each other plenty. She's fussing over having another girl around. She's hired a fancy restaurant to make us dinner tonight and she's hoping you'll go shopping at Ala Moana Center with her tomorrow."

"Why didn't you tell me? I didn't pack enough clothes to go shopping."

"Only a woman could say something like that. Don't you go shopping to *get* clothes? It's like a guy saying I don't have any fish in my freezer so I can't go fishing."

"No, you don't understand. You can't go…oh, never mind." By this time, a sleek white town car had pulled to the curb.

"Looks like our ride's here," said Ono. "You mind riding in back? I usually ride shotgun with the driver."

The driver turned out to be a three-hundred pound local man in a billowing aloha shirt that probably could've sheltered a family of four.

"Eh, *brudda*," the driver said, coming around the front of the car to fist-bump with Ono. "Lemme put your junk in the trunk."

Ono handed over his small valise and my overnight bag. While the driver was busy unlocking the trunk and stowing our gear, I cupped my hands against the dark tinted back windows and peered inside. I jumped a little when I made eye contact with a tiny face peering back at me.

"Oh! Sorry." I sounded as if I'd stepped on someone's foot.

"Hey, Tomika," Ono said, as he pulled open the rear door. "Sweet of you to come down here to get us."

Tomika slipped from the back seat and stood on the curb. She was only a bit taller than she'd been sitting down. She looked somewhat older than Ono—perhaps late fifties or even early sixties—but I sure as heck wasn't going to comment on their May/December romance.

She and Ono hugged long and hard. If I hadn't been a tad jealous of their obvious love for each other, I'd have found the scene touching.

"Tomika," said Ono when he finally pulled away, "this is my cabin girl for this weekend, Pali." He beamed as if he'd won me in a contest.

"*Aloha*, Pali." Tomika extended her hand, and gave mine a little squeeze. "It's my pleasure to have you visit my home. Your name, it means 'cliff' or 'steep hill' in Hawaiian. Do you know why your mother named you this?"

I wasn't about to go into the origin of my name—especially since it's a made-up name, not my birth name. "It's actually just a nickname from childhood. It also means 'difficult' as I'm sure you know."

"Ha! Ah, that is correct. I've known quite a few *keiki* who could have rightfully been named 'Pali'."

We got in and the driver ran around the car closing all the doors. Aside from four wheels and a roof, the plushy town car had nothing in common with my Geo. First of all, it smelled like Lemon Pledge, rather than a load of dirty laundry. Everything, from the electric windows to the multiple stereo speakers murmuring cool jazz, seemed in tiptop shape. The silky leather seats felt so comfy I was tempted to lean back and grab a few winks.

"Ono tells me you're a wedding coordinator. That must be exciting."

"It is, most of the time. Sometimes it's frustrating. People, especially brides and their mothers, think everything must be perfect. As if a flawless wedding day will make up for every slight, every disappointment, every loss they will face throughout their marriage. If the least little thing goes wrong, some of them come completely unglued."

"Ah, but it's supposed to be a celebration of love. A time for family and friends. In my experience some of my most charming memories are of things that didn't go quite as planned. That's the beauty of life, don't you agree?"

"Yes, but try telling that to a bride whose silk gown gets soaked by a rogue wave during the pre-wedding photo shoot."

"Well, regardless of the circumstances, I'm sure you do a wonderful job. And to always be working around happy people—people in love—you are truly blessed."

The lady put Pollyanna to shame. They ought to bottle her so I could take a snort every time I had to handle a hissy fit over flawed dyed-to-match shoes, or I had to referee a mother versus stepmother catfight over the reception dinner seating chart.

"Mostly it's a great job," I said. "But there are days when all I want to do is go home and spend a nice quiet evening with my own best man: Jack Daniels."

Tomika stiffened and pointedly turned to look out the window at the buildings flashing by. Call me paranoid, but I could've sworn the temperature in the car had dropped fifteen degrees.

# 9

Tomika Fujioka's condo was on the forty-first floor of a gleaming sky-blue high rise adjacent to the Ala Moana Center. I'm not keen on elevators, having ridden in them only a few times in my life, and zipping up four hundred feet in a matter of seconds didn't sit well with my empty stomach; but once inside her condo, the view from the floor-to-ceiling windows made the ride almost worth it. I guess if you're stuck living in a big city, this is definitely the way to go.

"It's spectacular," I said. She'd probably heard that more than a few times before, but there really wasn't another way to say it.

"Some gorgeous view, huh?" said Ono. "I'm not much for city-dwelling, but I make an exception for Honolulu. Look at that endless horizon. And the lights at night will knock you out."

Tomika came in carrying a black lacquer tray with a pitcher of fruit juice and a plate of exquisite French macaroons, those perfect little pastel cookies that look fake but melt in your mouth. I held myself back to avoid looking like a lion on a hyena carcass, but after I counted to ten, I snatched up a pale pink one.

"Aren't these just the sweetest little treats?" Tomika said, admiring the lemon-yellow cookie in her hand. Meanwhile, I was brushing the crumbs off my lips from the pink one that was by now long gone.

"Oh, come on," said Ono. "These are sissy cookies. I was hoping you'd get those chocolate chip ones from that shop in Ala

Moana. You know, the ones as big as hubcaps with the nuts and the hunks of chocolate."

"Ah, my brawny sailor-man," said Tomika. "Don't worry. I've got some of those for you in the refrigerator. I was hoping to first tempt your palate with these lovely French works of art."

"I don't want art," he said. "I want food." He got up and strode into the kitchen—a polished oasis of black granite and stainless steel—as if he owned the place.

I heard the refrigerator door open. "Anyone else want a real American cookie?"

We both declined.

He came back with an enormous cookie in hand, and sat down on the sofa next to Tomika. They looked at each other with such tenderness I averted my eyes.

"It's wonderful to have you back here," she said, patting his thigh.

"Great to be here. The crossing was pretty good. Kinda choppy going around Molokai, but that's to be expected. It took us just a little over twelve hours."

"Oh, I meant to ask you," said Tomika, "are you ready for the party, or do you need Bub to take you down in the morning to get things set up?"

"Nope, we're good. I told Pali you wanted to do a little shopping with her tomorrow, and if it's all right with you, I'm going to stick around here and watch some football."

"That's a good plan," she said. She rose from the sofa and started toward the kitchen, but then turned and looked at me. "You're not allergic to seafood, are you, Pali? I ordered some nice lobsters to be sent up."

"I love lobster. It's a real treat for us on Maui; we don't get it that often. Did you find some Australian lobsters at the market?"

"No, they're fine, but they're usually rather small. For company I like to buy the fresh Maine lobsters. More meaty."

"Well, you know what I like," said Ono.

"Yes, dearest, and so I'm having them send up some *ahi poke* for you along with the lobsters."

Personally, I'm not a *poke* fan. It's nearly sacrilegious to admit, because it's practically Hawaii's official state dish, but raw fish in any form: *poke, sushi, sashimi*, you name it, makes me want to spit it out on the floor.

"Oh, and I hope you like asparagus," Tomika went on, "I ordered some that they fly in from California. Very tender, and the cook dresses it with a lovely hollandaise sauce."

It pretty much went that way for the rest of the night. The china was Limoges, the glassware was Waterford crystal, and Tomika toted dish after lavish dish from the kitchen until I was worried I might have to unbutton my shorts in order to stand up. She didn't offer wine, but after twelve hours of wind-whipped sailing followed by the stress of being in her foo-foo big city digs, I would've declined anyway. By the time she served the coconut crème brulee I was only a blink away from dozing off.

Ono said he'd clear the table and she took him up on his offer. We adjourned to the living room to admire the twinkling lights of the city and finish our coffee. When Ono returned, he took a seat next to Tomika, and draped his arm across her shoulder.

She smiled at Ono, then me. "Pali, I'm giving you the front guest room. It has a beautiful view of the harbor. And you, my dear," she laid her hand flat against Ono's cheek and held his gaze, "will sleep in your usual place; right where I can keep my eye on you."

***

The next morning I woke up early. I lay in the soft bed wondering about proper guest etiquette for making coffee in someone else's home. Is it rude to sneak into the kitchen and rustle through her cabinets? Or is it considered polite to step up and not leave everything to Tomika?

After fifteen minutes of debating the issue, my need for caffeine settled it. I tiptoed to the kitchen in my tee-shirt and panties and quietly opened doors and drawers looking for coffee and filters. All I found were whole beans, which meant grinding, which meant waking up Tomika and Ono. I abandoned that idea and was slinking back down the hallway when Ono popped out of the bathroom. I gasped and pulled at the hem of my tee-shirt in an attempt to cover myself up.

"Sorry," he said, giving my legs a quick appraisal. "I didn't realize you were up."

"Yeah. I'll cop to my caffeine addiction. I can't do morning without a cup in hand."

He smiled. "You sleep okay?"

"Like a rock." I didn't ask him how he slept; it might open the door to more information than I could handle so early in the morning.

"I almost came in to check on you last night, but I didn't want Tomika getting the wrong idea."

I looked in his eyes. What was that about?

He nodded toward my room and continued. "You better put on a robe. Tomika's sort of a prude about flashing too much skin."

"I didn't bring a robe."

"Check in your closet."

I looked in the guest room closet and, sure enough, I found a lovely jade green silky robe hanging on a padded hanger. I slipped it on and was about to return to the kitchen when I heard voices in the hallway.

"Good morning, my sweet." It was Tomika.

"Good morning. How're you feeling? You get rid of that headache?" Oh yikes, the woman had feigned a headache? I wanted to clap my hands over my ears to avoid overhearing any more.

I opened the bedroom door and Tomika smiled at me. "Oh, how pretty that is on you with your lovely blond hair and blue eyes. You look beautiful in green." I guess some people don't need coffee to be cheery in the morning—or flattering. My hair's more dishwater than blond, my eyes more hazel than blue.

*"Mahalo,"* I said. After all, who was I to correct my hostess? "This is a lovely robe. Is it silk?"

"Yes. It's from southern China. I don't admire their politics, but they do make gorgeous heavy silks." She paused a moment, then continued. "I want you to have it."

Without coffee in me it took me a few seconds to respond. "Have this? You mean this robe? Oh, *mahalo*, but no. I've already imposed enough staying here with you and Ono."

"I insist. It's not every day I get to meet someone new and give them a little present. Please don't disappoint me."

I looked over at Ono. His head was down and he was rubbing his eyes as if he was still waking up, but it looked more like a ruse to avoid casting a vote on whether or not I should accept the expensive robe.

"Well, I don't know what else to say but *mahalo*. It's a very generous gift. I'll think of you every time I wear it."

"There, you see," Tomika said, turning to Ono. "I told you she was a nice girl. You would do well to surround yourself with nice friends like Pali when you're back home on Maui."

# 10

I'm not one for puzzling things out. I prefer the direct approach. Schemes, mind games and sarcasm don't work for me. I wasn't a hundred percent sure what was going on with Ono and Tomika's relationship but I figured I'd wait until we were back on the boat for the trip home and then I'd just come right out ask. I spent a pleasant Sunday morning with Tomika poking through the immense cathedral of commerce called Ala Moana Shopping Center, but I didn't buy anything except a new cell phone battery. As soon as we got back to her condo I installed the battery and my phone fired right up. The screen showed I had messages waiting, but I chose to ignore them until I could return the calls in private.

A few minutes after three we were in the town car headed back to the harbor. Bub pulled to the curb at Holomoana Street, across from the harbor entrance, and Ono and I got out. We trudged down to the moorage and I waited while Ono fiddled with the keypad on the metal gate, since getting to the actual dock required punching in a code.

"You and Tomika have fun today?" he said. We'd both been quiet on the ride downtown, as if each of us was waiting for the other to bring up the subject of Tomika.

"Yeah. She's a sweet lady."

"That she is. I probably should have clued you in on our relationship before bringing you over here."

"I, uh, well…" I was about to say something dumb, like it wasn't any of my business, or something equally phony. Truth was, I was dying to know.

"She saved my life. Literally. There's no doubt in my mind," he said.

I waited.

"Yeah, I was one sorry son-of-a-bitch when I showed up in Honolulu three years ago. When my wife Penny died, I didn't take it well. For one thing, I quit my job—or to be honest, I was fired. I'd started drinking pretty heavy, and the only way I could keep myself from putting a gun in my mouth was to keep pouring liquor in there instead."

I looked over at him, but he wouldn't catch my eye.

"It's hard to think about," he said. He stopped and put his duffel down. He stared toward the far end of the dock like he didn't have any idea what he was doing there.

"Hey, you don't have to go into the ugly details if you don't want to," I said.

"No, it's good for me to talk about it. I came to Hawaii on a whim. I think I blamed the dark and rain of Portland for my drinking and depression, so I figured if I moved someplace warm and sunny I'd snap out of it. Problem was, it didn't work out that way."

I nodded.

"Once I got here I started hittin' the booze even harder, if you can believe that. I had no friends; I lived in a ratty *ohana* shack I rented from a guy up in Waianae. I'd take the bus down to the city and get so drunk I couldn't figure out how to catch the bus back home. One night Tomika was out with some friends and I…" He paused and sucked in a breath.

He continued. "Wow, this is harder to talk about than I imagined. I don't usually unload on people like this. Sorry." He dragged his hands down his face.

"Hey, I'm serious," I said. "You don't have to air all your dirty laundry at once. I'm fine with just taking it one pair of socks at a time."

He smiled. "Yeah, thanks. But if you don't mind, I'd rather get it over with. I haven't told this story very often. They tell me it gets easier every time."

I wanted to tell him 'they' were usually full of crap, but I kept quiet.

"Anyhow, I panhandled Tomika and she gave me a fifty dollar bill wrapped around a business card. I couldn't believe it. Then she told me I could count on more where that came from if I'd go to the address on the card and call her when I sobered up." He smiled. "I had no intention of sobering up, and with the price of the rot gut I'd been drinking, fifty bucks was more than enough to kill me."

He went on. "Funny how stuff works, you know? I took that fifty and started walking toward an ABC Store. I was planning to buy the biggest bottle they had, but then I just kept walking until I got to a Christian mission down on Pau'ahi Street. That was the address on the business card."

I said nothing. It was tough for me to imagine this good-looking, energetic man panhandling and sleeping off rot-gut in a homeless shelter.

"Anyway, I got into a program and Tomika offered to be my sponsor."

"Isn't a sponsor usually another recovering alcoholic?"

"Yep. That's how it works."

Okay, picturing Ono as a pathetic alcoholic was one thing; picturing Tomika pounding down the booze took more imagination than I possessed.

"She was a drinker?"

"Yeah. When you've got money, it's even worse 'cuz it's a much longer fall before you hit bottom."

I nodded.

"I can't talk about her story, but trust me, she's got demons we wouldn't wish on our worst enemy. Saving people isn't a hobby for her, it's a necessity."

***

At a quarter to four, Chico showed up carrying two bulging plastic shopping bags of juice and gin. I watched as he set up the bar and wondered how Ono and Tomika felt about having all that liquor around.

The first guests began arriving at five. There were lawyers and real estate tycoons, business owners and politicians. I couldn't quite figure out what they all had in common, but it wasn't my job to scrutinize the guest list; I was there to make sure they had a good time.

After everyone was aboard and had a drink in hand, Ono fired up the engine and we pulled out of the harbor. We cleared the channel and were headed north, toward the Honolulu airport, when one of the male guests got up on the steps leading to the stern and bellowed for everyone's attention.

"I'd like to offer a toast to our hostess." He had to yell to be heard over the rising wind. "We've all benefitted from Tomika and Willie's generosity and I think I speak for everyone here when I offer my *ko'u mahalo* for your kindness, and wish you all the best in your retirement. The *Honolulu Press and News* will never be the same without you."

I looked over at Tomika, standing on the deck holding a glass of fruit juice festooned with the obligatory paper umbrella and cherry on a pick. She was looking down. When she raised her head, her eyes were shiny and her lips tightly clamped, as if she were walking a thin edge between sorrow and pride.

"*Mahalo* to all of you, my good friends," she said. "You have stood by me and my dear, late husband through all kinds of happy times and hard times. Your *aloha* and good wishes mean more to me than the most precious of jewels. My home is always open to each and every one of you. May you have the good fortune of a long and interesting life, and may each of your families be safe and prosperous for generations to come."

She may have looked like she was struggling to keep her emotions in check, but I couldn't have been that eloquent if you'd given me two days' head start.

We sailed up the coastline almost to Ewa Beach before turning around. It was dark when we returned to the harbor and the partygoers had become quiet. One by one they made their way off the catamaran, kissing and hugging Tomika while whispering their *mahalos* and best wishes. She left arm-in-arm with the last departing guest who'd offered to drive her home.

"Whew. That was fun, but I'm exhausted," I said as I picked up used plastic cups and appetizer plates and stuffed them into the garbage bag Chico held open for me.

"I think Tomika was amazed everyone showed up," said Ono. "We were pretty much at capacity." He sounded tired, but I chalked it up to the stress of keeping the boat on course and getting all those mucky-mucks safely back without incident.

We swept and wiped up and hauled trash for the better part of an hour. Then Chico slipped on his sandals and waved good-bye.

"We'll be pulling out no later than six," said Ono.

"Got it, boss. I'll be here."

While we waited for Bub to come down and pick us up, we made small talk but avoided revisiting the topic of Ono and Tomika's struggle with sobriety.

I was eager to get back to Maui. Back to home base and my normal life. But, as they say, be careful what you wish for: it wouldn't be long before I'd be hard-pressed to remember what normal life even looked like.

# 11

At five-thirty on Monday morning we were back in the town car and Bub was driving us back down to the harbor. The sun had barely lightened the sky beyond the Ko'olau Mountains and by the time we got underway the wind was blowing hard from the south. The crossing was rougher than it'd been on Saturday, but we still managed to make it to Lahaina before dark. Ono slipped the catamaran carefully alongside the dock and Chico jumped out and tied it up. As I gathered my belongings and picked up my sandals, Ono pulled two white envelopes from a drawer in the cabin and handed one to Chico, the other to me. Chico gave Ono a fist-bump thanks and bounded onto the dock. I hung back.

"*Mahalo* for thinking of me," I said. "I appreciate it."

"Are you kidding? You saved my ass. Chico's a good sailor but he's kind of lacking in people skills. And Tomika really enjoyed having you around. She told me so."

"I can't believe she gave me that silk robe," I said. "It's gorgeous."

"Believe me, she loved every minute. Maybe you'll consider going out with me another time?"

I nodded, unsure of what I'd just agreed to do.

As we said our *alohas*, I reminded Ono we'd be doing Keith and Nicole's photo shoot at nine on Saturday, right before the ceremony.

"I'll have everything spic and span."

"I guess I'll see you then," I said.

"Unless I see you before. Call me if you want." He leaned in and put an arm around my shoulder and gave me a squeeze. I'll admit to being a tad disappointed it wasn't followed by at least a peck on the cheek.

His comment about calling reminded me I hadn't picked up my cell phone messages for three days. I generally didn't get many messages on the weekends but it was unheard of for me to go incommunicado for more than a day when I had a big wedding coming up.

I punched in my voicemail code.

*You have six messages*, said the stern female voice. The number of messages and her surly tone made me feel even worse about falling off the radar for seventy-two hours.

The first two messages were vendors—the DJ and the bartender—confirming the date, time and place of the reception. I was known for getting cranky with my suppliers if they didn't call and check in with me a few days before a wedding. But it was justified. I'd literally been left standing at the altar without things like flowers and folding chairs, and once even the official performing the ceremony was a no-show, so I demanded a call-in from everyone the week before a wedding.

The third message wasn't a vendor. It was the guy who'd called on Halloween night—the night I'd been searching for Crystal. Same whispery voice, same peculiar accent. "So, I guess you don't take me for serious," he said. With his accent it sounded like 'cirrus'—a type of wispy cloud—but I was pretty sure he wasn't calling to discuss the weather.

He went on. "That's too bad, you know? 'Cuz I wanna talk to you. Don' keep me waiting too long, Ms. Moon, or you'll be sorry. Okay?" I heard muffled noise in the background, but I couldn't make out what it was. Bar clatter? A sporting event? I saved the message and went on to the next one.

Hatch's familiar deep voice came on after the voicemail lady announced I'd received call number four on Sunday at eight-twenty-three a.m. "Hey, Babe. I'm off today. You want to get together? Call me. I'll wait to hear from you." Oh, darn. I'd forgotten to call him and tell him I'd be out of town. Not good.

The fifth message was from Glen Wong. "Ms. Moon, we're wrapping up our investigation on your report of November One. If you'd like a hard copy of the final paperwork, give me a call. We've documented the damage to your vehicle for your insurance company."

The sixth and final message was from Keith Lewis. "Where are you? I came by your shop and then I called your home number. Your roommate said you'd gone out of town. We've got less than a week to go here. Call me—now."

I sprinted up Front Street, my anxiety level tipping into the red zone. The message from the creepy guy, me standing up Hatch on his day off, and Keith's continuing grumpiness made my homecoming feel less than welcome. The only good news was my car was right where I'd left it in the alley behind my shop. It appeared unscathed, so I didn't stop to check it over. Maybe subconsciously I wasn't prepared to deal with any more creepiness, especially now that it was getting late and the alley was in deep shadow. I walked right by, not even stopping to put my overnight bag in the trunk, and headed for the stairs.

In the soft glow of the setting sun I noticed something shiny and yellow hanging on the doorknob to my shop even before I started up the steps. Halfway up, I could tell it was a little Chinese silk pouch with a drawstring closure. Many of the local jewelers use them as gift bags when you buy a necklace or a pair of earrings.

Out of reflex I looked up and down the street hoping to catch sight of someone. A pang of guilt caught in my chest. Had Hatch brought me a peace offering for his recent lack of attention? Or maybe Keith and Nicole felt bad about their rude dismissal of my concerns about Crystal. Whoever it was, it lifted my mood to come upon an unexpected treasure. I shifted my overnight bag to the other shoulder and bounded up the last few stairs.

I carefully unwound the drawstring from around the door knob. The pouch was feather-light. I fingered the contents through the smooth silk. There was too much in there for it to be earrings or a simple gold chain. I imagined a shell necklace or maybe a coral bracelet. I don't wear much jewelry, but when I do, I prefer organic stuff—like shells or clay beads. Only Hatch would know that.

I unlocked the door and went inside. The room smelled like I'd left an egg salad sandwich on the window ledge for three days, but a quick scan of the room didn't turn up any misplaced foodstuffs. I dumped my overnight bag and the gift pouch on the desk and rummaged around for a can of tropical breeze-scented air freshener.

Outside, the light was failing so I flicked on lights as I sprayed. The yellow silk pouch gleamed in the glow of my desk lamp. I couldn't take it any longer. I pulled the puckered silk open along the drawstring.

Inside I saw a jumble of shells, but they didn't appear to be strung. I tipped the pouch and poured the contents into my palm. It wasn't shells. When I recognized what I was holding, I gasped and dumped it all out on the desk.

They were human fingernails. Entire nails, not just cuttings. They weren't bloody or torn so I figured they must be fake—probably acrylic. Each had hot pink polish and a tiny palm tree decal. I'd seen them before when Nicole had proudly shown off the matching mani-pedi's she and her bridesmaids had gotten the day of the bachelorette party.

My pulse thumped in my neck as I dialed the phone.

"Maui Police Department. Do you have an emergency?"

"No, I need to speak to Detective Wong. This is Pali Moon, returning his call."

"Please hold while I transfer your call." There was a click and then an earnest-sounding male voice came on to scold callers about the dangers of drinking and driving. After half a minute, he was cut off mid-sentence.

"Detective Wong."

"Hello, Detective. Pali Moon here. I've got something you need to see."

"Another donation for 'Locks of Love', Ms. Moon?" I heard the chuckle in his voice, but I let it go because once he realized what I had he'd be apologizing. He'd be hard-pressed to sell his Halloween prank theory now.

"No, what I've got here is even more disturbing."

"Before we waste my time and yours, why don't you just tell me what you're talking about."

"Fingernails."

"Fingernails? I'm afraid I'm not following you, Ms. Moon."

"I've got the missing girl's—I mean, young woman's—fingernails. They were left at my shop door while I was over in O'ahu."

I waited while he took a moment to connect the dots.

"Ms. Moon, I'm afraid I'm still not following you."

"What's to follow? Remember I told you about that bridesmaid who went missing on Halloween? Well, now we've got her hair *and* her fingernails. And besides that, I also have a recorded voicemail from a creepy guy who's threatening me."

"Where are you right now, Ms. Moon?"

"At my shop in Lahaina. I'm upstairs, above Hargrove's, the restaurant on the corner of—"

"I know where Hargrove's is, Ms. Moon. Stay right there. I'll be down within the hour."

So I had an hour to kill. I plucked up the fingernails and laid them out in order, like two phantom hands with the flesh missing. All fingers and thumbs were present and accounted for. I scooped them up and poured them back into the pouch. Then I listened to the four messages on the landline phone in my shop. Each was a check-in call from a vendor—the Plantation Inn confirming the reception date, Keahou confirming the cake delivery, the gal making the bridesmaids' leis, and finally, my roommate Steve announcing he was prepared for the photo shoot at nine on Saturday.

I called Steve on our home phone. When he didn't answer, I left a message telling him I'd made it back to Maui but I had a few things to deal with at the shop and I wouldn't be home for awhile. I thought about calling Hatch but decided against it. I didn't want to get into a long-winded discussion of my trip to O'ahu and then have Wong show up in the middle of it.

Finally, I called Keith but he didn't pick up. I left a message asking if he and Nicole could meet me at my shop at eleven o'clock the next morning. We'd go over the wedding schedule and discuss any last-minute concerns. I tried to sound as nonchalant as one can while staring at a pouch containing the ripped-off fingernails of a missing bridesmaid.

Wong made it in forty minutes. He managed to find the back stairs in the pitch black alley and was rapping on my shop door as I came out of the restroom.

I turned the latch and let him in. "Sorry I didn't leave the door open. I was so creeped out by the fingernails I locked up before going to the bathroom. Have you been waiting long?"

"Just got here." He looked around the cramped space. "This isn't as nice as your place up in Pa'ia."

I said nothing. To my knowledge he'd never been in my old shop on Baldwin Avenue. But Steve had told me Wong was the consummate busybody. Rumor has it on his time off Wong checks out people, places and things all over the island like a king checking the nether reaches of his kingdom. Steve said behind his back people refer to the detective as 'Peeping Wong'."

"Well, this is the best I can do for shop space right now," I said. "And it looks like I may be here even longer than I'd hoped. The Mo'olelo Society has decided to turn my old shop into a visitor center."

He nodded as if it was old news.

He pointed to the desk phone. "May I listen to the voicemail you reported?"

I walked over and picked up the receiver before realizing the sinister voicemail wasn't on my shop phone, it was on my cell.

"It's in there—on my cell phone," I said, pointing to my overnight bag.

Wong waggled his finger in a 'bring it here' gesture.

I rummaged through my bag for the phone and when I looked up, Wong's eyes were darting around the room, taking in everything.

"Nothing much escapes you, does it?" I said.

He shot me a half-smile, as if he wasn't sure if I'd meant it as compliment or criticism.

I punched in my voicemail number and entered my code. When the robot lady announced the time of the creep's incoming message, I passed the phone over to Wong.

He put the phone to his ear and I waited while the message played.

"What was the caller referring to—about being 'serious'?" said the detective. "Maybe it's a supplier you've forgotten to pay? Or maybe a potential wedding client? I don't hear the threat you claim to be hearing, Ms. Moon."

"The guy said I'd be *sorry*—that sure sounds like a threat to me."

"Well, maybe you'd be sorry to miss out on some new business. Or maybe it's a florist who wants to tell you about a great deal on orchids." He smiled a *there, there, little missy* kind of smile and I shot him some stink eye.

"Okay, if it would make you feel better, I'll run the number through our database and see what comes up." He listened to the message again, jotted something down in a little notebook he pulled from his shirt pocket, and then handed the phone back to me. "If it turns out to be anything significant, I'll let you know."

I opened my mouth, then closed it again. I reached over and picked up the silk pouch from the desk top and silently held it out to him.

He waved it off and pulled two latex gloves from his pants pocket. He snapped them on and took the pouch from me. Then he shook the fingernails into his open right hand. *Ha!* I thought, as I watched him examine the nails. *He's left-handed. Wong's not the only one with an eye for detail.*

"Okay, Ms. Moon, I'll take these in and see what we come up with. Until then, I'd appreciate it if you'd keep this to yourself."

"No problem."

Even though he'd been stingy with an apology for blowing me off last Thursday, his attitude change was reward enough. He returned the fingernails to the pouch and slipped it into a small plastic evidence bag he'd pulled from another pocket of his pants. He borrowed a black marker pen from my desk and wrote the date and time at the top of the bag. Finally he wrote *Lets Get M, Lahaina/P. Moon* on a large white square in the middle of the bag. I couldn't help but be impressed he remembered my business name, even though he shortened it and he left out the apostrophe in *Let's*.

When he finally left, my anxiety level dropped a notch with each of his footfalls on the outside stairs. I worked my jaw back and forth a couple of times to loosen it up. My concern over Crystal's welfare had been a heavy burden I was happy to hand off. The authorities had what they needed to start looking for her, freeing me up to concentrate on the task at hand: Keith and Nicole's fast-approaching Saturday wedding.

I locked up and skipped down the stairs feeling ten pounds lighter.

# 12

It was a little after eight when Wong left—not too late to call Hatch even on a night before he'd be going back on shift. Not even too late to drop by if he was around. I wanted to share my cheerful mood after being relieved of the Crystal dilemma.

Hatch picked up on his cell number after two rings.

"Hey, are you home?" I said.

"Yep, I gotta go to work tomorrow morning." His voice had an edge I hadn't noticed before.

"Can I come by for a few minutes? I won't stay long."

"It's a free country," he said. Then, as if he realized how snippy that sounded, he continued, "No really, come on over. I'll be up 'til ten."

Hatch lives in a swanky neighborhood called Sprecklesville. Not a very Hawaiian-sounding name, the area was established over a hundred and fifty years ago as a thriving sugar mill operation owned by "boss man" Claus Spreckles. Now the sugar refinery is gone, and what's left is a pristine beachfront community of multi-million-dollar homes. Hatch's cottage sits at the entrance to a sprawling property owned by an Australian film producer. The movie guy and his entourage show up a few times a year. The rest of the time Hatch pretty much has the run of the place. He'd become a de facto "boss man" himself, managing a small army of landscapers, housekeepers and maintenance people who troop through, day after day, keeping up the main house, three guest houses, two pools (salt- and freshwater) and assorted outbuildings and gardens. The property even boasts a heli-pad and an observatory complete with mini-Hubble tele-scope for stargazing.

As I was making my way through the West Maui hills, my cell rang. I'm usually good about not taking calls while driving, but I was concerned maybe it was the weird guy who'd left the threatening message. I didn't want to miss talking with him in person.

"Ms. Moon?" I was wrong, it was Wong.

"Yes, Detective."

"Good news. Our forensic tech worked late tonight and I was able to catch her before she left. I showed her those fingernails. Seems they're fake. She said they're called 'silks,' made from a silk fabric which is applied over a woman's natural fingernails. Manicurists use them to strengthen the living nail and make the fingernails stronger and appear longer. They're easily removed with acetone and are believed to be easier on the nail bed than acrylics."

*Did he call to give me a beauty school lesson?*

"Anyway, I think the prankster is still just messing with you," he said. "Are you sure you can't think of anyone who might be behind this? Maybe someone who's faking foul play to get you to drag the police department in on the joke?"

He didn't wait for me to answer before going on. "You know, if we had any cause to believe this was for real, we'd be hard at it. But seventeen years on the job tells me we've got a practical joker here. You see what I'm saying?"

"No, I don't, Detective. A woman is missing. Whether the hair and fingernails are for real or fake doesn't change the fact that Crystal Wilson vanished nearly a week ago."

"We've gone down this road before, Ms. Moon. Right now we're working at least a dozen complaints involving visitors.

We've got some who racked up big hotel charges using phony credit cards. We've got abandoned rental cars. We've got one case that's similar to yours where the so-called boyfriend took off and left his girlfriend stranded here with no money and no plane ticket home. Tourists pull the disappearing act all the time."

"So that's it?"

"For now. But don't hesitate to call if something new turns up." He said it the same way a shop clerk would chirp *Have a nice day*.

I turned off the Hana Highway at the sign marking the entrance to the Maui Country Club. Then I made a sharp left into a leafy lane that winds around the backside of the golf course. Hatch was sitting on his front lanai when I pulled up. He gave me a wave and pointed to a spot where I could park the Geo. When the owner was in town Hatch liked me to park out on the road, preferably a block or two out of sight of his landlord. Not that the TV producer was a prude about Hatch's love life; I think it had more to do with the aesthetics—or lack thereof—of my trashy-looking ride.

I got out of the car and took a deep breath. This area smelled like the exact opposite of my funky shop over the fish restaurant. Here, the wind carried scents of plumeria, gardenia and freshly cut grass. The hush of on-shore waves beyond the foliage was accompanied by lungfuls of oxygen-rich ocean air.

I approached the cottage and Hatch's Jack Russell-mix pup came charging through a hole in the screen door and out onto the lanai in a hail of high-pitched barking. Wahine—the Hawaiian word for 'lady'—never let physical barriers slow her down. She'd been known to leap from a moving boat to take a swim, and once she'd chewed through an inch-thick rope in mere minutes when he tried to tie her up outside.

"She thinks getting tied up is like working a Sudoku—it's just a puzzle begging to be solved," Hatch had said.

When Wahine clearly saw me, or smelled me, or whatever means she used for ID'ing humans, she abruptly stopped barking and her tail went into overdrive.

"Hey, sweetie." I bent down and rubbed her chin, then moved to her chest, while she attempted to lick every trace of sea salt residue from my neck. I'm not a dog-person, per se, but I make an exception for 'Heen', Hatch's shortened-up name for her.

When I looked up, Hatch was waiting for me on the lanai. He was holding two wine glasses—white for me, red for him.

"Bed," he said in his daddy voice, and Heen trotted over and plopped down on a wadded-up blanket near the door.

He kissed me lightly on the lips, then handed me my wine.

"When you didn't call me back yesterday I thought maybe you'd decided to dump me but forgot to clue me in," he said. His voice was teasing, but in the meager glow of the yellow bug light I noticed a tight line across his forehead.

"No, I'm sorry, I was working. You know that guy, Ono, whose catamaran you recommended for this weekend's wedding? Well, his cabin girl got sick so he asked me to help out with a gig he had over in Honolulu."

Hatch raised his glass and took a long time, sniffing and swirling. He was no wine connoisseur, and chances were good the wine had come out of a box, so I figured his sommelier act was more a stalling tactic than an attempt to impress me with a newfound interest in oenology.

"You have a good time over there?"

"It went fine. I stayed with the woman who owns the boat. She's a really nice lady, and her condo is spectacular. She even gave me a silk bathrobe." Okay, I was laying the gender thing on a little thick, but I didn't want him leaping to conclusions about the sleeping arrangements.

"I thought we had a date for Sunday. You didn't even bother to call and let me know you wouldn't be around."

"Again, I'm sorry. We left really early Saturday morning and then the weekend just sort of flew by."

"But I called you Halloween night and told you I would be off on Sunday. In fact, I left you a bunch of messages."

I only remembered one message, but I was already in the wrong so I didn't want to quibble. "I'm sorry I didn't get back to you. It took a day to get over there and then we had to get ready for the party, and then it took another day to get back. All I can say is I'm really sorry."

He started the wine swirling thing again.

"Look, Hatch. I don't know what else to say except 'I'm sorry.' You've been busy, too—going out fishing and all. Can't you just accept my apology? It wasn't as if I didn't call you on purpose."

"So, what'd you think of Ono Kingston? Quite a guy, huh?"

I know a loaded comment when I hear one. "He's fine. He keeps the boat really clean and he's a good sailor. We made the crossing to O'ahu in about twelve hours."

"Did you get seasick?"

"Not really. I kind of liked the rockin' and rolling."

"Oh, I'm sure you did. And I'll bet he did too." By now my eyes had grown accustomed to the dark and I couldn't miss seeing his clenched jaw working a muscle in his cheek as if he were chewing cud.

"What's wrong with you? If you have something to say, then say it. I've already apologized for not calling. But I earned two hundred bucks for helping out with a boat party for the owner's business associates. That's it. If you're implying it was anything more than that, then say so."

"Pali, Pali." He said it as if he was talking to a kid caught playing with matches. Hatch had been a cop for seven years before switching to firefighting. He acted liked a fireman but often still thought like a cop.

"What, Hatch?" I sounded cranky, but I'd groveled enough.

"I don't have a problem with you doing stuff on your own. You're free to come and go, no problem. But in the case of Ono Kingston I feel kind of responsible for your safety since I'm the guy who gave you his name."

"My *safety?*"

"Look, I don't want to dis him or gossip or whatever you call it in Hawaiian—"

"*Ka'ao.* Gossip is called *ka'ao.*"

"Anyway, it's just that although he seems like a stand-up guy, there's more to his life story than meets the eye."

"You mean about his drinking?" I felt a twinge betraying Ono's confidence, but I wanted to put the brakes on Hatch's holier-than-thou lecture before it really got rolling.

Hatch downed his wine. He crossed the lanai, settling into one of two sling-back chairs set on either side of a massive square ottoman. He pointed to the second chair in an unspoken offer for me to join him. I weighed my options.

"C'mon," he said after a few moments. "I'm the good guy here. It won't kill you to hear me out."

I plopped into the chair and put my feet up. The *shush-shush* of waves rolling in on the nearby beach tempted me to close my eyes and drift off. I was beat after the long day of sailing. If I hadn't been obliged to stick around as payback for blowing him off on Sunday, I'd have given Hatch a peck on the cheek and gone home. Instead, I braced for a sermon.

Hatch had only gotten a few words out when a wide-body jet on final approach to Kahului airport roared overhead. It was so low I could count the tires on the extended landing gear. The deafening din of the turbine engines rattled our wineglasses on the side table. As Farrah would say, the airport noise was *karma* in action. The swanky community sits smack dab in the flight path, only a few miles from the main runway. Usually, the planes come in from the other direction, over the cane fields. But when the wind shifts, they switch and come in over Sprecklesville. Each of those wide bodies is bringing in tens of thousands of mainland tourist dollars, so the locals' calls for noise abatement procedures mostly fall on deaf ears. As the Maui Tourist Board likes to remind us, *it's not noise, my friends, it's the sound of full employment.*

"As I was saying," Hatch continued. "Overall, Ono's a good guy, but he's got a dicey side. I've heard some things. Just make sure you don't find yourself alone with him when other people aren't around."

I wanted to laugh. Doesn't *alone* pretty much mean that other people aren't around? But years of martial arts training had taught me to keep my emotions—and my smart-ass remarks—in check. I kept quiet.

We sat in silence for a long minute.

"Okay," he said. "I know, it sounds like I'm jealous or something. But that's not it. I swear."

Again, I didn't respond.

"You see," Hatch went on, "Kingston was a hot-shot architect over on the mainland, used to getting his way and having other people clean up his messes. Then his wife died and the guy went nuts. The doctor who'd misdiagnosed her cancer died from poisoning three days after her funeral. The police had Kingston in their radar, but they couldn't prove anything. Then, he started drinking, which I guess he told you about. But he wasn't just drinking. They were investigating him not only for the poisoning but for drug dealing, smuggling, all kinds of crap. Trust me, he may keep a clean boat, but he can be one unstable dude."

"Hatch, I appreciate your concern, but it's unnecessary. First off, we were never alone. The first mate, Chico, was there when we were out on the catamaran, and then when we got to O'ahu we stayed at the owner's place and she was home the entire time. So, even if he had nefarious plans in mind, he had no opportunity to act on them. Okay?"

Now it was Hatch's turn to be silent.

"I've got to get going," I said. I stood up. "I've got to check out limo drivers in the morning, and then I've only got four more days until the biggest wedding I've done in months."

Again, he played the mute card.

"Okay. You want me to thank you for giving me the heads-up on Kingston? Fine. I'll be careful. But in return, I need you to accept my apology for not calling on Sunday."

He nodded. "I'm working tomorrow but you can stay over if you want." It sounded less like an invitation than an attempt to clear the air.

"*Mahalo*, maybe next time."

I crossed the lanai and turned back and looked at him. More than anything, I wanted to ask his opinion of Crystal Wilson's disappearance, along with the hair, the fingernails, and the creepy voicemails. I'd been so relieved when Wong had left with the fingernails, but then he'd snatched away that good feeling with his last call. Maybe if Hatch heard me out and agreed with

Wong that it was probably all a joke I could shake the nagging feeling I should be doing something about finding her.

"You got something else you want to say?" Hatch's tone let me know I was in jeopardy of overstaying my welcome.

"No, I'm just tired. I need to get to bed before I fall over."

"Take it easy up on Baldwin." He said, his voice softening. "Scanner's saying they've got a DD checkpoint set up near the Hana Highway intersection."

"*Mahalo.* I'll be careful."

***

Steve wasn't around when I got home. I didn't bother checking to see if he was upstairs, but went straight to my room, stripped off my clothes and crawled into bed. The wine, coupled with very little food all day, was working its magic on my usually racing thoughts. I was asleep before I knew it.

The next morning I awoke at five. Usually, I roll over and get my best sleep of the night until the alarm goes off at seven-thirty. But I couldn't drop off again. I tossed and turned, plumping the pillow and flipping it over for about a half hour before giving up. A beautiful young woman was out there, in the dark. Someone had chopped off her hair and ripped off her fake fingernails. Worse, from the looks of things, I was the only person on the entire island who gave a damn.

# 13

At six a.m. I pulled into a parking spot behind the Palace of Pain. For me, the best antidote to stress is an hour of kicking and screaming. I hadn't been down there for a while and I expected some ribbing from Sifu Doug, my kung fu instructor and the owner of PoP, but when I arrived he wasn't there.

I let myself in using the key I'd been given when I'd earned my first black belt. No matter how recently Doug had cleaned, the PoP always smelled the same: sweat and grimy feet. I kind of liked it. I imagined that's what my dad would've smelled like after a hard day at work. But I'd never know what my dad smelled like since he'd hot-footed it back to the mainland when I was just a baby. My mom died before I was old enough to ask her if she had any idea where he'd gone.

I flipped on a single light switch. There were four rows of fluorescent bulbs, but I preferred the cool, cave-like ambiance of just one row to the blazing in-your-face glare Sifu Doug insists on while teaching classes. I warmed up by going through my entire repertoire of forms. I usually skip the easy ones and get down to business, but I paid penance for my recent absence by starting at Form One and doggedly working my way up the line.

Around seven, my sifu showed up.

"Hey, call the cops. We got alien intruders in here!" Doug grinned and switched on the rest of the lights.

"*Aloha*, Sifu. I figured I better get back down here before you took my picture off the wall."

He turned toward the display of portraits of all the black belt fighters who trained at PoP. "You still up there? I tol' them to take you down *months* ago."

He came across the mat and we did a quick, but complicated handshake routine that included fist-bumps, palm slaps, and so on. It was one of those things the guys took very seriously but I never did. Nevertheless, I'd worked my way into acceptance and I wasn't about to blow it over some Mars versus Venus thing.

"What's with you skipping practice?" he said. "I was gonna call and nag you, but I ran into Steve at the market and he said you been real busy working on a fancy wedding."

"Yeah, I have. But it'll be over on Saturday. I promise I'll get down here more often after that."

"Good. Well, I've got some paperwork I need to catch up on. You're still planning on coming next Monday night, right?"

I hesitated. I'd completely forgotten Monday's promotion ceremony.

"Uh, sure. You need me to judge?"

"No, I've already got the judges lined up. But I like to have all the black belts here to observe. It means a lot to the little guys."

"How many are up for promotion?"

"Twenty-three. White to brown." That meant it would be an hours-long ceremony, mostly little kids. And, with brown belt as the highest level, pretty boring. But there was no way I'd gripe to my sifu.

"Wouldn't miss it."

"Great. Well, I'll let you get back at it. Good to see you, Pali. We miss you when you're not around." I felt a pang of remorse for staying away so long. Then it hit me. Doug was one of the most solid guys I knew—a happy family man, former

Army Ranger. He was highly disciplined and no-nonsense. If he smelled a rat, it was time to bait the traps.

"Doug," I said. Doug turned, his eyes squinting at me as if I'd whispered *help*. I rarely addressed him by his given name and he seemed to sense I wasn't going to ask for tips on stance or breathing.

"What's up? You got some trouble?"

"I don't know." I asked if we could talk in his office for a few minutes. "I promise I'll keep it short."

"No worries. I'd rather blow off this paperwork for a while anyway."

I went through a quick review: finding the hair on Halloween; my trip to the police station; the bridal couple dismissing Crystal's disappearance because she was a flake; the fingernails hanging on my doorknob and, finally, Wong's claim that the whole thing was a prank. When I finished, I blew out a breath.

"That's it?" he said.

"Pretty much."

"Have you talked to Farrah?"

I nodded.

"What'd she say?"

"She did a tarot reading for the bridal couple and didn't like the groom much. I showed her the hair before I gave it to Wong and she said it gave off a really bad vibe. I think her words were 'feels to me like that missing girl's in deep doo-doo'."

"Yeah? Well, I vote with her."

"So, what should I do?"

"I think you know what you should do, but you don't want to do it."

"Story of my life."

"Story of everybody's life," he said with a smile. "That's why we kick major ass around here."

***

It was coming up on eight o'clock when I turned into the alley behind my shop. I'd spent the entire commute to Lahaina fussing over what to do about Crystal, and I wasn't any further along than I'd been in Pa'ia. I parked as close to the wall as I could to block entry to my passenger-side door with the broken lock. I pushed down the locks on the other doors before heading upstairs. The smell in the alley seemed pretty tame and I hoped the atmosphere in my shop would follow suit. I'd be leaving in less than an hour, though, so no biggie.

I turned the key in the door and, as I entered, I checked the desk phone to see if the message light was blinking. It wasn't.

My appointment with the limo service was at nine, and the place was only fifteen minutes away. I busied myself getting the coffee all set up, everything ready to go, for my eleven o'clock meeting with Keith and Nicole. I considered going over to Star Market to pick up some pastries, but nixed that idea. It'd be better to treat them to lunch downstairs at Hargrove's. A rather expensive gesture, but I figured I needed to haul out the lavish to make up for not getting in touch with them all weekend.

I pulled up to Napili Limo at nine on the dot and Manny waved me in past a snarling Doberman. He held the dog's collar while I got out.

"You need that beast to keep out intruders?" I said.

"I keep him for show. I don't want nobody messing with my cars. But he don't bite. Never has. I think if some guy showed up with a mess of jerky ol' Duke here would let him drive a limo right on outta here." He scrubbed the dog's ears, and the Doberman nuzzled his hand for more.

"Can I see the cars you've got lined up for me for this weekend?"

"Sure, no worries. I saved the best ones for you."

I looked around the scrubby dirt lot. There were three limos—two white, one black.

"I ordered four," I said.

"Yeah, I know. I got one getting the tires rotated."

"C'mon, Manny. Don't mess with me. Where's the fourth one?"

He shook his head. "Cracked up. My brother takes it out for one night and manages to run off the highway down by Puamana. Tore the shit out of the undercarriage." He grinned. "But don' you worry, I got an uncle up in Wailuku. He's got a nice van. Real clean. He offered to ride your people."

"Manny, these are rich California people. They can tell the difference between a minivan and a limo."

"But it's real nice. Kind of a dark red. Got chrome rims— the whole nine yards."

It was too late for me to find something else. I'd have to mention the van at today's meeting with Keith and hope he'd go along with it.

"Okay, Manny, but I'm not paying limo prices for your uncle's *keiki*-van ride. Half."

"Half? No way. The gas is the same, the wear on the tires the same, and I gotta pay the driver for the same amount of time."

"The driver's gonna be your uncle, right?"

"Yeah."

"Then he gets half. If he's smart and he shows them a good time maybe he'll get a nice tip. But I'm not paying a hundred bucks an hour for a Wailuku minivan, nice rims or no. Fifty bucks—tops. And I want you to shave a little off the others because you promised me four limos and you're only giving me three."

He stared at me; I stared back.

"God, you're a mean *wahine*. I try to make a living here, you know? I got two kids, and this dog here eats like a third kid. It's not easy, dude."

I was getting perturbed. "Look Manny, when your *brudda* smacked up your limo you should've called me and told me what was up. I don't like surprises. Especially last-minute surprises. Now, do we have a deal or not?"

"How about ninety bucks for the others and seventy-five for the van?" he offered.

"How about I take my business someplace else?" I started for my car, aware that if Manny let go of that Doberman, he might get to see his dog bite someone for the very first time.

"Okay, okay. Seventy-five for the limos, fifty for the van."

"And who's going to be driving?" I said.

"I drive the bride and her girls; my *brudda* Kane—he's not the one who did the crash, that's my other *brudda*—drives the groom with the guys. I'll get my sister's husband, Larry, to drive the third limo and then my uncle will bring over the van. Sound good?"

I'd worked with everyone he'd mentioned except the Wailuku uncle. "Can I call your uncle and talk to him beforehand?"

"Sure. He works swing, unloading barges at the Kahului wharf. But you can call him in the afternoon—around four o'clock, before he has to be at work."

Terrific. Today I get to tell Keith that not only is he not getting the four limos I'd promised, but the replacement van will be driven by a day-sleeping longshoreman.

I gave Manny his deposit and got a receipt. I went through the timetable with him and warned him of the consequences for being even ten minutes late.

"Whoo-ee, you one hard-ass lady," he said. "I don't know why you pound on me so bad. Have I ever let you down?"

I made it back to the shop by ten-thirty and, again, parked close to the wall to prevent anyone from getting into my car through the unlocked passenger door.

By ten-forty, the coffee was perking and I'd fought back the downstairs kitchen smells using my arsenal of odor fighters.

I pulled out the Keith Lewis/Nicole Johnson wedding file to scan for any overlooked details while I waited.

At eleven-ten, I got up and peered out the window to see if Keith and Nicole were cruising for parking. Except for my Geo the alley was empty, with at least a half-dozen open spots going begging.

I called their cells but in both cases it went directly to voicemail. I left the same message on both phones: *Hi, it's Pali. I'm hoping you're on your way down for our meeting today. Everything looks good. I just want to go over the final schedule with you. See you soon!*

When the minute hand on my desk clock clicked on the six for eleven-thirty, I started pacing. Up to that point Nicole and Keith had never been late for a meeting and I was feeling the weight of not returning Keith's call from last weekend. What if something had come up with Crystal and they'd needed my help? What if Nicole or another girl had also gone missing? I plopped down in the guest chair and put my head in my hands.

Sifu Doug had said I knew what I needed to do. Problem was, I didn't. I only knew how I felt. And how I felt was worried. Worried and sick at heart.

# 14

No sense sitting around waiting for the bridal couple to show up. It was nerve-wracking and I'm not a patient person. Better to drive up to the Ritz and see if they'd overslept—or if they hadn't checked their cell phone messages and weren't aware I'd asked for the meeting.

I locked up and went down to the alley. My car had a folded piece of paper stuck onto the front windshield. No biggie. Every few days I get a flyer on my car. Usually it's for things like outcall massage, an all-you-can-eat luau, or a timeshare solicitation with a *fantastic* offer of a free sunset cocktail cruise in exchange for only ninety minutes of your vacation time.

I plucked the paper from under the windshield wiper and flipped it open. The handwriting was in a childish print, black ballpoint pen. *We got the girl. $500,000 US or she dies. No cops. Tell him he nows were to send the money.*

Aside from the obvious misspelling of 'knows' and 'where' and the reference to the money in US funds, the note provided few clues as to who'd written it. I called Wong on his cell but it immediately went to his voice mail. Then I took off for the Ritz, hoping against hope Keith and Nicole might have some answers.

I parked in the upper lot and made my way down to the lobby. At the desk, I asked the clerk to ring room number 2371.

He picked up the house phone and put his hand over the receiver, "And your name is?"

"Pali. Pali Moon."

"Oh," he said, putting the phone back down. "I believe we have a message for you." He flipped through a box with tabs marked with room numbers. "Yes, here it is." He brought out a bulging cream-colored business-size envelope with my name written on it and the Ritz Carlton logo thickly embossed in the upper left corner next to the return address. I wasn't sure if I was supposed to tip him or not, so I settled for flashing a big smile and offering a sincere *'Mahalo'*.

I asked if Keith Lewis was still registered at the hotel. The clerk tapped on his keyboard, paused, then tapped some more. He stared at the screen, then tapped the 'enter' key about ten times. I wondered if he was messing with me for not offering a tip or if locating a registered guest really required that many keystrokes.

"It says here he checked out this morning. At eleven thirty-two. Our normal checkout time is eleven, but since Mr. Lewis was in the Hanalei Suite, we allowed his party a little leeway."

*In other words*, I thought, *you'd already extracted an obscene sum of money from him so why quibble over an extra half hour.*

"And the others in his party? Have they checked out as well?"

"Hmm. Let me see. His file shows he was responsible for six additional rooms. It'll take me a moment to review the status." He typed. And typed.

"Yes, the entire Lewis party departed this morning and the bill is paid in full. Is there anything else I can help you with?"

I turned and noticed a line had formed behind me.

"No, *mahalo* for your time."

I wandered into the lobby wondering if Keith had run out on me without paying. If so, I'd be kicking myself for years to come. Most couples provide me with a credit card to pay their expenses, and then I present them with an invoice on the day of the wedding—a detailed receipt for their records even though their card has already been charged. Keith had been unwilling to give me a credit card. Instead, he'd offered a three thousand-dollar retainer with a promise to pay the bill in cash the day before the wedding. The retainer, along with his pricey on-island address of the biggest suite at the Ritz, had convinced me he'd be good for it.

Now I felt like an idiot for not demanding a card. I sat down heavily in the same comfy chair I'd occupied when I'd met with Keith the previous Friday. I carefully unsealed the flap on the envelope. The envelope was so chubby I wondered if he'd enclosed photos or maybe a rambling letter of excuses for ditching at the last minute.

Before I could allow myself to look at what was inside, I calculated my situation. The Lewis/Johnson wedding expenses were already at nearly five thousand dollars, even before the seventy-five-dollar-a-plate wedding dinner and the two-thousand-dollar photo shoot. Keith had given me three thousand, which meant I'd need more than five thousand to come out whole. I'd owe at least three thousand in cancellation fees and non-refundable costs like the printing. I shut my eyes and took out the contents of the envelope. Right away I could feel it wasn't photos or pages of Ritz-Carlton stationery; it was cash. I clutched the wad in my fist for a few seconds, conjuring up good vibes. I vowed that if Keith had made me whole on the money I owed, I'd donate any extra to charity.

I looked down at the money. It was a thick wad—all hundred-dollar bills. I flicked through the stack, then looked up, wondering if it was wise to be flashing so much *kala* around in a public place. I shifted in my seat, allowing me to count the money while hiding it between my hip and the upholstered arm of the chair. It took me nearly five minutes to count it and then count it again.

***

The ride back to Hali'imaile ended up taking less than an hour but it felt like an eternity.

"Hey, what're you doing home so early?" Steve said looking up from reading the morning paper. "You've got some messages over there by the phone."

"I'll bet one of them is from my buddy, Keith Lewis, blowing off his wedding this Saturday."

"What? No, he didn't call, and when I talked with him yesterday he seemed rarin' to go. He even asked if we could maybe move the bride's photo shoot up to Friday."

"Well, they didn't come to their countdown meeting this morning and when I went up to the Ritz to find out what happened, the entire wedding party had checked out."

"Sounds like maybe Ken and Barbie got cold feet. But at least you're covered with his credit card."

"He didn't give me a card."

"Whoa, I thought you always got a credit card."

"Normally I do, but in this case he insisted on paying in cash. He gave me a three grand retainer when we signed the contract, and promised to settle up the rest on Friday. But I'm okay. Look what he left me at the hotel desk." I reached into my beach bag purse and pulled out the Ritz Carlton envelope. I removed the cash and fanned it out on the table.

Steve's mouth gaped open. "Wow, how much you got there?"

"Ten thousand bucks."

"Did he owe that much?"

"No, he owed only about half that. Once I pay my people and take my commission I'll still be ahead almost four grand."

"Are you giving him a refund?"

"I'll offer if I hear from him, but for now it seems he's in the wind. I've left three messages on his cell and he hasn't called back. The only mainland address I have is a post office box in Del Mar, California. Which brings me to my next problem. Look at this." I handed him the paper I'd found on my windshield.

"Holy crap, Pali, this is a ransom note!"

"Yeah, it sure looks like it. I left Glen Wong a voicemail but I haven't heard back from him yet."

"Pali, this is serious. They could be torturing that poor girl right now. I think you should call the police station and tell them you've got an emergency. Make them track Glen down immediately."

He was right, of course. Sometimes I don't trust my emotions. I'd learned long ago to tuck them away where they couldn't bite me in the ass. But I'd been fretting over Crystal for almost a week. Finding the fingernails and then the ransom note had ramped my fret level up to near full-blown panic, but panic was an emotion I'd been taught to disregard. For me, panic was right up there with crying. It's okay to *want* to do it, but not okay to *actually* do it.

# 15

Nobody likes getting interrupted in the middle of something, but since Wong worked homicide, he was probably used to it by now.

"What's it now, Ms. Moon?" he said when he called me four minutes after I'd called the station number on his business card. "I'm going to have to turn my phone off in a couple of minutes so this better be good."

"I got a ransom note."

"A ransom note," he echoed. "And what does your 'ransom note' say, specifically?"

"You want me to read it to you?"

He blew out a breath that came across the phone line as a loud *whoosh*.

"Okay," I said. I motioned for Steve to bring me the note and I read the four short lines to Wong. "Notice how he mentions US money. Oh, and although I read you the words 'know' and 'where,' he actually spelled them wrong. He left out the 'k' in 'know' and he left out the 'h' in 'where.'"

"What's going on with you, Ms. Moon? Why are you still messing around with this? I was dead serious when I requested that you not concern yourself further with official police business."

"Look, Detective, I'm not enjoying any of this. I don't know why I was picked to be the go-between with all of this stuff, but I was. I'm concerned about the welfare of the woman they're referring to in the ransom note, that's all."

"Ms. Moon, I'm about to board a flight to Honolulu on official business. But in the interest of showing good faith I'm willing to reschedule my trip on one condition: you promise to hand over the note and leave this entire case up to us. From this point on, I don't want you snooping around, or telling kidnapping tales to your kung fu buddies. Do I have your word on that?"

"Absolutely. Look, I've got my own problems, Detective. My big Saturday wedding's been cancelled. The only people I'll be talking to are my suppliers when I call to pull the plug."

"Huh, so that wedding got cancelled. Do you know why?"

"No clue, the bridal couple just up and left."

"When?"

"What do you care? You said yourself this whole bridesmaid thing was a hoax."

"Ms. Moon, I'm going to have to call my boss and rearrange my schedule in order to deal with your situation. I'd appreciate you granting me the courtesy of straight answers."

"Okay, right after the ransom note was put on my car I went up to the Kapalua Ritz where they were staying and they'd already checked out. I don't know why they left or where they're going, but they paid me what they owed and they won't take my calls, so I'm assuming that's the end of it."

"My plane's already left without me. Give me a minute to clear things up with my superiors and I'll come up there and get your so-called ransom note. Stay right there. When I arrive, be prepared to tell me *everything* you know about this situation so we can put this thing to rest." He hung up.

"Wow, what a grouch," I said to Steve. "I don't know why you think that guy's so hot."

"I didn't say he was 'hot.' I said he was—oh, forget it. So, what's going on?"

"Well, mister hot-or-not Glen Wong's coming up here to get the note. And—I'm quoting here—'put this thing to rest.' Not one word of concern about Crystal."

"He's probably playing it close to the vest," said Steve. "Doesn't want you to get a big head 'cuz you've brought him something important after he blew you off before."

I shrugged.

"No, think about it," he went on, "they're gonna have to start taking Crystal's disappearance seriously now. They'll probably call in the FBI or something."

Steve and I sat in the living room until Wong's car pulled into the driveway. When Steve got up to go to his room, he put a hand on my shoulder.

"Let the police handle this, Pali. Don't make it your problem."

I nodded. I'd promised to butt out, but that didn't mean I wasn't going to do everything in my power to keep tabs on their efforts to find Crystal and bring her back unscathed.

Outside, two car doors slammed shut. I peeked out the window. Wong had brought along a partner.

"Hey," I said to Wong as I opened the door. "It's just a sheet of paper. Probably won't require two of you guys to haul it out of here."

"Pali Moon, this is my partner, Detective Bert Konomanu." Konomanu was holding a soft-sided briefcase with both hands. He bobbed his head in greeting.

"You any relation to Noni Konomanu?" I'd gone to school with Noni, but she was no longer a friend. It had to do with her trying to steal my business earlier in the year.

"Yeah, she's my cousin on my dad's side. She's living over in Honolulu now, working for Tank Sherman."

I invited them in and offered them something to drink. Both asked for water. I went into the kitchen to get the water and pick up the ransom note. The cash was still fanned out on the table. I gathered it up and stuffed it in my purse.

"Nice house," Wong said as I came back to the living room. "How long you been living here, Ms. Moon?"

"A couple of years. Why do you ask?"

"No reason. We're supposed to put the public at ease by starting off with small talk. It's part of the chief's new 'customer service' program." He turned to Konomanu as if expecting him to contribute some idle chit chat of his own, but Wong's partner stared straight ahead—silent.

"Okay, then, let's get down to business. May I see the note?" Wong pulled a pair of latex gloves from his pants pocket and snapped them on his hands. Konomanu did the same.

"I'm afraid I've been handling this paper all morning," I said. My voice came out in a panicky tone I hadn't expected. "I mean, my fingerprints are probably all over the thing."

"We watch *CSI*, Ms. Moon. Our technicians can deal with ruling out known prints. Your fingerprints are still on file from the last time you called us for help."

"Oh. Okay."

He carefully opened the folded note and leaned over so he and his partner could read it at the same time. Then Konomanu extracted a plastic bag from his briefcase and held it open while Wong dropped the note inside. Konomanu sealed the top and then took out a felt pen and wrote on the bag. He carefully laid the bag on top of a stack of papers already in the briefcase. Wong and I watched the whole procedure in silence.

Before zipping the briefcase closed, Konomanu yanked off his gloves and Wong did the same. They stuffed them in their left pants pockets. Then they both took out notepads and ball-point pens from an inside pocket of their jackets and clicked the pens at the same time. They'd obviously been partners for some time—it was like watching a tightly choreographed Cirque-du-Soleil *pas de deux.*

"Okay, let's begin," said Wong.

Two hours later I wearily closed the door. I'd told them ev-erything I could remember about Keith and Nicole, even throw-ing in Farrah's claims of bad auras and chilling tarot readings. After they left, I felt even more ill at ease. I flipped the lock on the door. Strange—the last time I'd been careful to lock my front door was the first time I'd ever met Detective Glen Wong.

***

The next morning, I drove to Lahaina anticipating the mis-erable task of notifying my vendors that Saturday's wedding had been cancelled. I made a list, and prioritized it by who needed to know first. Keahou topped the list since she typically started making her cakes three to four days before the wedding. The guy I'd signed up to perform the ceremony brought up the rear. He used a fill-in-the-blanks script and typically showed up only a few minutes before the start time. His contribution was rarely moving or eloquent, but he was a plus-size local guy, with the big *kahuna* look that Keith and Nicole had insisted on.

I clomped up the back stairs to my shop and unlocked the door. The fish smell didn't seem as robust as it sometimes was, but maybe I was just getting used to it. When I got inside, the light on my answering machine was blinking. The first two calls were vendors checking in, and the third call was from Trish, my prospective December bride. *"Hi wedding lady! You must really be a busy gal. Seems we're playing phone tag here. Anyhow, I need to talk*

*with you about me and Buddy's Christmas-time wedding. Call me."*
She left her number.

I started dialing Trish's number, then checked my watch and realized it was five o'clock in the morning over on the mainland. As eager as Trish seemed to lay claim to Buddy, a crack of dawn phone call probably wouldn't be appreciated.

I dialed Keahou instead.

"Hey, girl," she said before I could launch into my no-go speech. "I was going to call you this morning. Don't worry, I got everything ready. I special ordered those nice papayas from the Big Island and they came in yesterday. They're perfect. Oh, and I already baked the groom's cake. Komo says it's my best boob job ever."

I told her the groom had cancelled the wedding.

"Oh, too bad. He dump her or she dump him?"

"I'm not sure what's going on. They took off before I could talk to them. But don't worry, he paid me. How much do I owe you?"

"Hey, stuff happens. *Mai hopohopo*—don't you worry about me. Do you want some Big Island papayas? I got two dozen here, and Komo and me will only be able to eat three or four before they go *hauna*."

I insisted on paying her for the groom's cake and for the twenty papayas she'd had flown in from Hilo. She refused any money for her time and trouble.

"You the one paying for this crazy boobie cake, then you should be the one eating it," she said. "When can you come and get it?"

I promised I'd drive up to Kula before noon. Then I went on to the next call. By ten o'clock I'd talked to everyone on my list. My cancellation charges totaled almost nineteen hundred dollars. Even after rounding it up to two grand, I still had a whopping five thousand dollars left over.

I convinced myself it was okay to keep at least some of the money. After all, when I'd made my pact to donate the excess to charity I'd never dreamed it would be so much. I settled on giving half to a worthwhile cause and putting the other half in my skinny savings account. After all, wasn't *I* a worthwhile cause?

Unfortunately, as everyone knows, nothing good comes from broken promises. As Farrah would say, *bad karma is way worse than bad luck*. Looking back, I wish I'd handed the entire ten grand over to the local women's shelter or the food bank and paid my vendor expenses out of my own pocket. Maybe if I hadn't tried to scam the universe I could've headed off a lot of what was about to unfold.

# 16

The ride up to Keahou's bakery in Kula was peaceful even though my mind was going a hundred miles an hour. Had Keith somehow known about the ransom note? Was he worried whoever snatched Crystal might later come for Nicole? How much did he know, and more importantly, what would the kidnappers do to Crystal now that he'd taken off?

"There you are," Keahou sang out as I peered through the window in her kitchen door. "*E como mai*—come in, come in." She'd boxed up the groom's cake and had a big paper bag, bulging with the almost-ripe papayas, ready for me on the table.

"You hear anything from your bridal couple?" she asked, gesturing for me to sit down while she cut a thick slice of cinnamon bread and placed it on a plate before me.

"Nah. They're long gone, probably on their way back to the mainland. I don't even have a home address for them."

"Huh. What address did they put on their marriage license application?"

I looked up from buttering my bread. "That's what's strange. They used a post office box number. Almost like they didn't want anyone to know where they lived."

We talked for about ten minutes and then the timer went off on her stove. "Oh, I gotta get that out of the oven," she said. "Komo's niece's boyfriend is having his twenty-one birthday and I'm baking a cake for the party."

"Busman's holiday, huh?"

She squinted at me. "No, I think he sells ads for **KPOA** radio. Not a bus driver."

I considered explaining the goofy expression, but then thought better of it. Besides, I needed to pick up the absurdly expensive bridal gown Nicole had left behind. The seamstress had been none too pleased to hear the bride had abandoned it, and she'd sounded nervous about getting paid. I'd promised to bring her the money and pick up the dress, but I had no use for it—my garage was already bursting with cold-feet castoffs from "Let's Get Maui'd." Farrah was always buying and selling stuff online, maybe I'd ask her to help me find it a good home on Craigslist or e-bay.

I picked up the pink cake box with one hand and hefted the bag of papayas in the other. "*Mahalo* for being so nice about this, Keahou. It seems I'm always cancelling on you. This is the third time this year."

"Oh, these things are hard to see coming. It's better they decide not to do it then go ahead and be sorry later, eh?"

"Yeah. But I wish they wouldn't wait until the last minute."

"This not last minute. Last minute is like what happened to my sister's sweet baby girl. You remember her—my niece Kulakai? Anyhow, her man says he has to go to the *lua*—how you say, 'the john'—ten minutes before the wedding supposed to start and then he beat feet right on out the back door of the church. That was stinky thing to do. Kulakai still spits on the ground when anybody say his name."

She pecked me on both cheeks and I returned it. Then I went out to my car and slid the cake box onto the backseat. I still couldn't look at that seat without seeing the ghost of Crystal's hair draped across it. Now that the ransom note had surfaced, looking at it freaked me out even more.

The clock in my car said twelve-thirty, which meant the work day had begun on the West Coast. I called Trish's work number and she picked up.

"Hey! Thanks for calling me back," she said. "Guess what? I'm leaving for Hawaii tonight. I talked my boss into letting me go to this swanky conference in Honolulu. Can we meet some-time to talk about my wedding?"

"Uh, well, Honolulu is on the island of O'ahu, not Maui. Any chance you could fly over here? I could show you around and we could start sketching out ideas." I prayed she'd say *yes*; I wasn't in the mood for another quick trip to Honolulu.

"I thought Hawaii was a state."

"It is."

"But isn't it, like, connected?"

"No, it's a group of islands. There are seven major islands and a bunch of tiny islands. The only way to easily get from one island to the other is by plane." I couldn't believe I had to give her a geography lesson. This is how Canadians must feel.

"How long does it take to get to Maui from Honolulu?"

"It's a short flight, less than an hour total. And planes leave Honolulu all the time. It's kind of like taking a bus. You just buy a ticket and get on the next available flight. By the way, where do you live on the West Coast?"

"I'm in Portland. The Oregon Portland, not the one in Maine," she said. I resisted telling her I could've figured that out since Maine was definitely not West Coast and, unlike her, I'd managed to stay awake in school during social studies class. Instead, I said, "Great. When you arrive, give me a call and we'll set up a time. I'm looking forward to meeting you."

We signed off and I checked the clock on my dash. Not quite one o'clock. I still had Keith's money in my bag and I needed to get to the bank. But the little chunk of cinnamon bread I'd had at Keahou's had whetted my appetite. I turned at Hali'imaile Road and headed for home.

I walked in the back door and Steve met me in the kitchen.

"You know, you really ought to hire a secretary," he said, handing over four scraps of paper with scribbled phone numbers. I quickly scanned the messages—none were from Keith.

"But why would I do that? You're doing such a great job."

"Don't push me, Pali."

"Tell you what. Since you've been so helpful and we haven't had any fun time lately, why don't I take you to lunch at Hali'imaile General Store. It'll be my Secretary's Day treat."

"I think it's called Administrative Assistant Day now. Is that today?"

"Probably not. But you deserve something nice for holding down the fort."

"Well there's nice, and then there's fabulous. Are you sure you can afford to take your 'secretary' to a gourmet lunch like that?"

"Yep. My 'administrative assistant's' been very patient with me, and I can't think of a better way to enjoy a little of this cash that's burning a hole in my pocket."

We went out to my car and I drove the short distance to Bev Gannon's famous Maui restaurant tucked alongside the two-lane road that cuts through the Hali'imaile pineapple fields. The place actually used to be the company store when the surrounding fields were sugar cane, not pineapple. The street view doesn't do justice to the delights that lie within. It's a simple clapboard building, with a tall false front, painted beige with white trim.

Wide wooden steps lead to a generous front porch. Once you step inside, you can feel the love. Vibrant sunny yellow walls sport colorful fish sculptures, and dozens of local art pieces are on display on tall shelves behind the bar. The palpable attention to detail assures diners they aren't there just to enjoy a great meal—they're also going to be treated to a few hours of pure *aloha*.

Two and a half hours later we left, giddy from the luscious lunch and two glasses of wine apiece.

"You okay to drive?" Steve asked.

"Probably. But why don't we walk home, just in case? We can be there in less than fifteen minutes."

We didn't talk much on the walk home, and once we got inside, we headed to our respective bedrooms. I don't know what Steve did, but I needed a few winks before heading back out to pick up my car. When I awoke, it was already getting dusk outside—time to start dinner. The bank in Pa'ia had been closed for more than an hour.

***

The next morning the phone rang as I was getting out of the shower. I hoped Steve would pick it up, but he didn't. When I heard the message on our kitchen answering machine kick in, I dashed out of the bathroom and snatched up the extension. The caller was already leaving a message.

"...hope you can come and get me. I'll wait for—"

"Trish, is that you?"

"Oh hi, Pali. Sorry to bother you at home. I tried your work number and your cell but you didn't answer, so I looked up your home number. I'm over here on Maui now. Can you come get me at the airport?"

"I thought you had to attend a conference in Honolulu."

"Oh yeah, that. Well, that's the story I gave my boss. If I sign in and show up for a few sessions, he'll never know why I really came over. The conference goes on for three more days, so I've got lots of time to make an appearance."

"What type of work are you in?"

"I see dead people."

I waited a beat.

"No, really," Trish went on with a chuckle in her voice, "I'm in the funeral services business. I'm a licensed embalmer and mortuary cosmetologist."

"Really?"

"Yeah, sounds kinda weird, huh? But the pay's great, and I'm really good at it. In fact, I won first place in the accident victim restoration category back at school. I enjoy putting people back together. It's sort of a joke around town that I'm the 'go-to girl' for the serious Humpty Dumpty cases."

No way was I going to comment on that.

"I live only ten minutes from the airport," I said, eager to change the subject. "Tell me what you're wearing, so I'll be able to recognize you at baggage claim."

"I'm wearing black. I'm always in black. Pretty much goes with the territory."

In New York City that wouldn't be much of a tip-off. But on Maui, a woman dressed in head-to-toe black would stick out like the proverbial sore thumb.

I parked in the hourly lot on the airport loop road and skittered across the street to the terminal. I stepped into the baggage claim area and scanned the crowd, searching for Trish. I spied her standing next to the far baggage carousel, wearing a forlorn look and sporting more black than the Wicked Witch of the West. Black pleated pants, a plain black blouse and a three-button black blazer. A black hobo-style purse was slung over her shoulder. She was standing next to a small black roller bag.

I waved at her and she reached down and grasped the handle of the roller bag. While she was making her way across the open space, I spied a former federal co-worker from my TSA days. It was Lenny Williams, a Drug Enforcement Agent. He was holding the leash on a beagle sniffing its way through a row of unclaimed luggage. I smiled at him and he nodded.

I started walking toward Trish. So did Lenny and the beagle.

When we got within speaking distance, Trish spoke first. "Wow, you're way younger than you sound on the phone," she said.

What'd she mean by that? Did my voice quaver? Was it too soft or too low? I wanted to ask her how my voice sounded 'old' but by then Lenny and the beagle had stopped in front of us. The dog stiffened, then barked a couple of times—loud—before resolutely sitting down on its haunches.

"Is this a cadaver dog?" Trish said in a stage whisper to Lenny. "I work with the deceased. It's impossible to get the smell out of my clothes."

Lenny ignored her.

"May I see your bag, miss?" he said, pointing at my beach bag purse.

"Lenny, it's me—Pali Moon."

"Miss, I'm asking for permission to search your handbag."

"For crying out loud, Lenny. I've only been off the job a couple of years. It's me, Pali. You know, the air marshal who flew the Honolulu to Taipei route?"

Lenny's face told me he sure as heck remembered me, but he wasn't going to let on.

"Sure, officer, I have nothing to hide," I said. Perhaps because Lenny knew I'd worked for Homeland Security he'd selected me to assist in a training exercise for the dog. I'd been involved in my fair share of phony scenarios while I was on the job, so it made sense I'd be his logical choice.

I handed Lenny my bag with a wink.

"I'm really sorry about the delay," I said turning to Trish. "My car's parked right across the street."

"No problem. I'm in no hurry," she said.

"Do me a favor, Lenny," I whispered. "Don't dump everything out where everyone can see it. I'm going to the bank today to deposit—"

Lenny held up a hand to halt my little speech. Then he lowered my purse to the dog's nose level so it could get a good sniff.

The beagle went berserk.

# 17

Lenny rooted around in my bag and pulled out the Ritz Carlton envelope. When he lifted the envelope flap and saw the large bundle of cash inside, he looked over at me slack-jawed.

"Miss, I'm gonna have to ask you to come with me," he said in a tone that sounded like a recording.

"Lenny, wait," I said. I turned and touched Trish's arm. "There's been a mistake. Would you mind waiting here for a few minutes? I'll be back as soon as I can."

"Can't I just go with you?"

"No," said Lenny. "I'm taking her into federal custody. No visitors allowed."

Not good. Not good at all.

"Just have a seat over there," I said to Trish. "I'm sure this won't take long once I answer their questions. I'll call you on your cell when I can—"

"Excuse me, Miss," Lenny said, interrupting. "But the security detail has alerted to contraband in your handbag. You need to come with me *now*."

*The security detail?* Sorry to break it to you, dude, but it's not a *detail*—it's a dog. And a rather scrawny little dog, at that. But, of course, I kept my opinion about the dog's lack of stature to myself. I'd seen enough training videos of federal agents dealing with uncooperative suspects to know it'd be best for me to keep my mouth shut and my feet moving.

We got to the back of the baggage claim area and Lenny punched in a code on a locked door. Then the three of us—

Lenny, me, and the beagle—went inside. The tiny room was furnished with a small rectangular table and two metal chairs. No window, no art on the walls, no cooling breeze from a fan. It wasn't the kind of place you'd want to hang out in on a coffee break. By now, the beagle appeared almost sleepy calm. The only sign of vigilance was in its eyes—it kept them resolutely trained on its handler as if anticipating a yummy reward.

"We'll wait here for the proper authorities to arrive," Lenny said, setting my bag down in the middle of the table. "Have a seat."

My cell phone chimed. Lenny shook his head and I let it go to voicemail.

I sat down and leaned over to pet the dog, but Lenny jerked the lease, pulling Fido out of my reach.

"It's illegal to touch a federal officer," he said. "Oh, and I'll need to see some ID." He pointed to my purse. "Do you have a driver's license or other identification in there?"

I nodded.

"May I look?" he said.

Again, I nodded. He dumped the contents of my purse out onto the table. The dog twitched as if it was dying to launch into its *gotcha* routine all over again, but it stayed quiet.

"Where'd you get so much cash?"

"It's payment for services. I'm a wedding planner and this is the money I was paid to put on a rather expensive wedding this weekend."

"Do you usually conduct your business in cash?"

"No, my customers usually use a credit card."

"Would you remove your ID from the wallet for me, please?" His tone was softening. Maybe his memory was slow on the uptake and he was finally recalling we'd once been colleagues working side-by-side at this very same airport.

I pulled my driver's license out of the wallet and handed it to him. The cheery rainbow on the license was the only spot of color in the stark white room.

"Pali Moon. You still live on Makomako Street in Hali'imaile?"

"Yes."

Just then, a DEA supervisor arrived. Lenny left the dog to keep an eye on me while he and the supervisor left the room. They huddled outside the half-open door. I caught snatches of their conversation, but couldn't hear enough for it to make any sense.

I glanced down at my cell phone on the table. The caller ID just showed a number, and I wondered who'd called. I picked up the phone and was punching in my voicemail code when the door swung open. I snapped the phone shut.

Lenny led the other guy into the room, but the supervisor did all the talking. "We're going to be impounding the contents of your purse for further testing," he said.

"Why?"

"It caused the security dog to alert for drugs."

"Drugs? What kind of drugs?" I looked at the stuff spread out on the table. Jumbled along with my wallet and the envelope stuffed with hundred-dollar bills was a tiny Kleenex pack, a plastic hairbrush with most of the bristles missing, and a smattering of tattered business cards from Napili Limo, Steve's photography business and a few other vendors I use in my business. "If I have any drugs in here, it's most likely going to be Tylenol or Advil or something like that."

"The security dog's trained to alert for opiates, marijuana, and methamphetamine," the supervisor said. "Not Tylenol."

"Am I under arrest?"

"You're in custody and will be taken down to the local police station. We really can't say much more than that right now."

"What about my personal property? As you can see, I've got a lot of cash here."

The two men exchanged a glance. "I don't think you should count on getting the money back, Ms. Moon. It's the primary reason you're going downtown."

***

I waited in a little interview room at the Wailuku Police Station for nearly half an hour before anyone showed up to talk to me. Then a guy came in and handed me a can of Diet Pepsi. "I'm Sergeant Bremmer, with the Hawaii Narcotics Enforcement Division. How're you doing?"

"As good as can be expected, I guess. But I need to make a phone call."

"Lawyer?"

"No, a wedding client. I was picking her up at the airport when I got detained by the feds. I need to call her and let her know what's going on. Although I don't know exactly what *is* going on."

"Tell you what," he said. "How about I get someone to call your so-called client to let her know you won't be meeting with her today? You can write her number down here." He pulled out a business card, flipped it over to the blank side and slid a pen across the table.

I wrote down Trish's name and number and he picked up the card and left.

When he got back he said, "Your client said she'll call you back when she can. I told her you'd be here a while longer and she said in that case she's heading back over to Honolulu. She sounded kinda nervous to me." He eyed me as if hoping I'd blurt out a confession that I'd been at the airport to score a big drug deal and, what the heck, why don't I give you the real name of my 'so-called client' so you can bust her before she gets on that plane for O'ahu.

"Great," I said." So, I've probably lost a wedding client over this. Are you going to tell me what I'm accused of?"

"In this room I'm the one asking the questions. But, to show good faith, I'll make an exception just this once." He smiled that brittle smile cops flash when they pull you over for fifty in a thirty-five. "Here's the deal, Ms. Moon—mind if I call you Pali?" He didn't wait for me to respond before going on. "You showed up at the airport this morning carrying a large amount of cash reeking of cocaine. You caused quite a stink—pardon the pun— with the drug-sniffing dog."

"Cocaine? That money was payment for a *wedding*. I've got the invoices to prove it."

Again with the snarky smile.

"We've had a chance to talk with Detective Wong," he went on. "We know you've been consorting with a person of interest who's been on our watch list for quite a while now. So why don't you tell me more about how you came to be in possession of ten thousand dollars that's so saturated with drug dust we're going to have to give our canine officer the rest of the week off so he can recover from nasal fatigue?" He chuckled at his own lame humor.

"Look," I said. "I run a legitimate business. I own a wedding planning service that coordinates destination weddings for mainland clients. I don't do background checks on my customers. If I was paid with drug money, then I'm as horrified as you are. But I have no idea where that money came from, I swear."

"You look like a nice person, Pali. And believe me, we want to believe you. But in order to give your story that ring of truth we're seeking here, we'll need some solid information. When Detectives Wong and Konomanu took your statement about your wedding client...what was his name again?"

"Are you talking about Keith Lewis?"

"Yeah, I guess that's the name he used. Anyway, they were less than impressed with your candor. So now it's my turn. We're going to go over every single detail of everything you know about this Mr. Lewis, and when we're through, if I feel you've been truly forthcoming with me, you can leave. How's that sound?"

"Sounds like a complete waste of everybody's time. I didn't hold anything back when I talked with Wong and his partner. I really doubt there's anything more you can wring out of me."

"Still, I'd like to give it a try."

And so began four hours of questions about every aspect of Keith Lewis. By the time I was excused I was exhausted—and starving.

On my way out, a police clerk handed me a plastic Ziploc bag. Inside it I could see my driver's license, my cell phone, and a piece of paper detailing the items they'd kept as evidence.

So—I'd walked into the Wailuku Police Station owning a beach bag purse containing a few personal items and a huge wad of cash. I walked out four hours later carrying a clear plastic bag that held my phone, my ID, and a voucher for ten thousand bucks I'd never see hide nor hair of again.

# 18

A street cop drove me back to my car at the Kahului Airport. When I asked if the police department would validate my parking, the guy laughed. I tried to convince the female lot attendant to cut me some slack because I'd spent the last five hours in police custody.

"What'd you do, *sista?*"

"They accused me of having drugs in my purse, but I didn't."

"Drugs? You packin' drugs? Girl, you don't get no sympathy from me."

"I didn't *have* drugs. The sniffer dog was wrong."

"You know it costs like a million dollars to train one of them drug sniffin' dogs. They're smart. Way smarter than *some* people."

I rooted through the glove box and managed to come up with enough cash to pay the full parking tab. Then I popped the clutch and screeched my tires getting out of there.

Although it was one of Hatch's non-duty days I didn't feel like calling him. He'd already gotten cranky about my little voyage to Honolulu with Ono. I wasn't in the mood to listen to a lecture about how I could've avoided today's events by vetting my customers a bit more carefully.

I called Farrah but I had to leave a message. She must've been with a customer. I hadn't seen her in so long I was sure she would have picked up my call if she could.

Next, I called Sifu Doug. "Hi," I said in the sunniest voice I could muster. "Where are you?"

"I'm home. Laila's at the grocery store and I'm watching the kids."

"I was afraid of that."

"Why? What's up?"

"I need to talk to you. I'm kinda in a jam. Can you meet me at the PoP in a little while?"

When he didn't answer, I went on, "I'm sorry to break in on your family time. If you want, I can come up there." Doug's house was further up the mountain, in Pukalani.

"No, I'll come down. I'll get the neighbor to watch the kids."

"I wouldn't ask if it wasn't an emergency."

"I know. See you down there."

***

After I caught him up on the events that landed me in an interrogation room at the Wailuku Police Station, Doug's forehead was deeply creased. "Pali, this is so weird. You know the other day when you told me about finding that hair and the fingernails and all that? Well, I put the word out. A day later my cousin Beni calls and tells me he needs a place to lay low for a while. He says if I take him in, he'll tell me what he knows about a red-haired *haole* girl who got herself messed up with some guys he hangs with. But my Laila put her foot down and said 'no way' would she let him come stay with us. Beni's been busted for drugs a bunch of times and even did some prison time over in Waipahu for dealing ice."

As he talked, the hair on the back of my neck prickled. Pretty bridesmaid Crystal Wilson was mixed up with local drug dealers?

"Yeah, so anyway, that's weird, huh?" he said. "You think Beni might know something, or is he just scamming me for a place to stay?"

"Only one way to find out."

***

About an hour later—just after five o'clock—my phone rang. "I'm afraid I don't have good news, Pali. Beni's pretty whacked out. Says he won't tell me anything until I promise him a place to hide. He can't stay at PoP because I've got classes to-morrow morning. And Laila's totally shut me down on him stay-ing up here at the house—even for just a night. Says she hates to turn away *ohana* members, but she's afraid for our kids."

"I can't blame her." I thought it over for a couple of beats. "You know, if he promises to behave himself, maybe I could put him up for a night or two. I don't have any kids, and I really want to hear what he has to say."

"You sure you want my doper cousin on your couch? I bet your roommate's not gonna vote for that."

"I'm not too crazy about it either, but I can't let this go. Even if Crystal's a druggie, or involved with druggies, she's still a human being. I won't be able to live with myself if I don't at least try to find out what happened to her. The police don't seem to be doing much."

I agreed to pick up Beni at Palace of Pain in half an hour. When I got there, he was hiding in the men's bathroom. I'd met Beni a time or two before, but the guy who came slinking out of the men's room looked nothing like the fresh-faced local boy I remembered. This guy resembled the wasted dude on the local "Ice Kills" posters. Skinny—real skinny—with a fringe of greasy dark hair shielding his eyes. The hair, as well as the rest of Beni, looked like it hadn't been washed in a month. His complexion was a mess; his teeth and gums even worse.

"Nice to see you again," I said, lying through my own twice-daily flossed and brushed teeth.

"*Da kine*, whatever," he said.

The ride back up to Hali'imaile was quiet. Beni slumped in the passenger seat, his face turned toward the passenger window. He lifted his left shoulder and kept it there in a feeble attempt to put a physical barrier between us. I had a bad feeling Steve was going to refuse to pay me any rent for the time Beni spent with us. If I hadn't had to hand over Keith's drug money to the police I'd have readily agreed. As it was, I was hoping we could work out a negotiated settlement.

Beni's move-in was a breeze. He travelled light, as in he didn't have a single thing. No change of underwear, no toothbrush, nothing at all. I took him upstairs to the guest room and opened the fold-out sofa. The thin mattress curled up on both ends. It looked about as comfy as a prison cot.

"You going to be okay up here?" I said.

Beni nodded. It was impossible to read his expression through the shank of oily hair.

"I'll bring up some towels and stuff so you can take a shower. The bathroom's right next door. You'll be sharing it with my roommate, Steve."

He shrugged.

"Are you hungry? We're going to have dinner in a little while. You're more than welcome to join us."

Head shake.

"Well, if you get hungry later on, no problem. Just come down and I'll make you a sandwich or something."

A shrug.

"Okay then, I'll go downstairs and get your linens."

Steve had come into the kitchen and was taking things out of the refrigerator to start our dinner. I didn't look forward to informing him he'd be sharing his upstairs living quarters with an unwashed drug-addled dude with the vocabulary of a mime.

*\*\*\**

Beni didn't come down for dinner on Thursday night, and he didn't come to breakfast the next morning, either.

"What's with this guy, Pali?" said Steve. "It creeps me out to be sleeping down the hall from a guy I've never even seen." His heaping bowl of health food store granola looked like it contained about as much fiber as a sheet of plywood.

"He's in hiding," I said. "Sifu Doug says Beni's scared there's a nasty drug dealer after him. But who knows? Paranoia and meth are like peanut butter and jelly. I'm giving him a little time to settle in and then I'm going to pick his brain about Crystal Wilson."

"Assuming he's got any brain left to pick."

"Yeah, he's kind of a mess."

At ten a.m. my patience ran out. Beni had been in my house for almost sixteen hours and I still hadn't even heard him use the bathroom. Maybe he'd gotten folded up in the sofa bed.

"Beni?" I rapped on his door.

No sound from inside.

"Beni, I have a key that unlocks this door. If you don't answer me right now, I'm going to assume the worst and come in to save you." I didn't really have a key, but sometimes a fib works wonders.

I heard shuffling across the wooden floor. Then the door opened a crack. The smell made me wonder if he'd rigged up a chamber pot rather than leave the room.

"Beni, I need to talk to you. Or, more precisely, you need to start talking to *me*."

"Whaddaya want to talk about?" His voice was slurred.

"Beni, have you been drinking?"

He laughed a feeble, choking laugh and opened the door a bit wider. Then he turned and flopped face-first onto the rumpled sofa bed.

The room was dark with the bamboo shade pulled tightly down. It smelled like rancid oil and human sweat.

"What's going on? You don't eat, you don't take a shower. What is this? Did someone take you to see *Psycho* when you were at a vulnerable age?"

"Huh?" He coughed a shallow, but wet, cough. "Hey, you got anything? You know—weed, pills, somethin' like that?"

"No, and even if I did I wouldn't give you any. We have a deal. You can hide out here for a little while, but you have to tell me what you know about the red-haired girl."

"Oh shit, man. I don' want to talk about that—not never!"

"Look, the only reason you're here is because you told your cousin Doug you'd tell what you know about her. I need to find her. If you've changed your mind, say so. Because if you're not going to honor your side of the bargain then you'll need to leave— like immediately."

"I can't talk right now. I'm coming down, eh? Give me a little more time, man."

"*Coming down?* Coming down from what?"

"You name it. I snorted some ice yesterday and it's ugly, man. Then I smoked some stuff—hash, I think. But it coulda been somethin' else." He held out a hand that shook like a palsied ninety-year-old.

"Okay, we'll talk tonight. But here are the rules of the house: you need to take a shower no later than three this afternoon and you'll come down for dinner at six."

"I'm not hungry, man."

"I didn't say you had to *eat* dinner; I said you had to clean up and come *down* to dinner. We got a deal?"

He nodded and put up a hand to wave me away.

"Oh, and one more thing. When you take that shower, use soap. And shampoo. I'll bring you some clean underwear to put on after."

"Dude, I don't wear no underwear."

"Well, *dude*, you will while you're staying here with me."

After I left, he slammed the door closed behind me. I stood in the hall trying to decide if I should steal a pair of Steve's old skivvies or politely ask him for some loaners. Common courtesy won out.

"No worries," said Steve. "I'll get you a couple pair. Just one thing: they only go one way. Under no circumstances whatsoever are those shorts welcome back in my room."

\*\*\*

It was just shy of eleven o'clock—plenty of time to drop by and visit Farrah before the lunch-time rush, but when I arrived she was midway through ringing up a big order. I gave her a wave and turned to leave.

"Hey," she called out. "Come back in a little while. I need to talk to you."

"Will do."

Now what? Going home to babysit Beni while he detoxed wasn't an option I'd even remotely consider. I ticked off the days of the week and realized this was Friday, a work day for Hatch. I could run by the station and say 'hi' and maybe gain a few points. I hadn't talked to him since our tiff over Ono, and I needed some sympathy for all the crazy stuff I'd been through in the past few days.

I pulled in at the fire station and parked in the visitor spot.

"Hey, Pali," said Mona, the stout local gal who served as receptionist, dispatcher, and self-appointed mother hen. "Where you been, girl? We don't see much of you 'round here lately."

"Oh, I had a big wedding going on this weekend."

"*Had?* Sounds like it's not going on no more." Nothing gets by that woman.

"Yeah, it got cancelled. The bridal couple had to go back to the mainland."

"Too bad. You want me to call *brudda* Hatch out here? He's in back with the guys. They just rolled in from a medical call about twenty minutes ago."

The only reason to call Hatch out front was so she could listen in. "*Mahalo*, no," I said. "I'll just go on back there. I can only stay a few minutes anyway."

She scowled as if I was breaking some kind of rule, but ever since Maui Fire began hiring female firefighters, the day room wasn't the sacrosanct 'man cave' it had been in earlier times.

She picked up the intercom and announced me. I may have danced away from her chance to eavesdrop, but she still wanted me to know who ruled the roost.

"Hey, babe," Hatch said, holding the door to the day room open for me. "What're you doing here?"

"Just dropped by to see you for a few minutes. Mona said you just got back from a medical call."

"Yeah, we got this old lady up in Papohaku who calls every week or so claiming she's having a heart attack. But her EKG's are always spot-on normal. I think the only thing wrong with her heart is it's broken. Lost her husband back in April."

"That's too bad."

"Yeah. Well, one of the guys is thinking about fixing her up with his great-uncle. You know, maybe have him pretend he's delivering pizzas and he's lost or something. He could go by her house and ask how to find a phony address in the neighborhood. Then she'll tell him there's no such place and he'll say they might as well eat the pizza together because there's no way he can deliver it since he doesn't have a good address. Then he'll go inside and she'll get him something to drink and they'll start talking. Next thing you know, no more phony heart attack calls. How's that sound?"

"Sounds like you guys are watching too much Lifetime Channel."

"Hey, it costs Maui County hundreds of dollars every time we haul her to the hospital for tests. We gotta do something." He motioned for me to take a seat on one of the battered sofas in the day room. Four guys in station blues were huddled around a computer in the far corner.

"What's this I hear about you getting in trouble out at the airport?" he said.

So much for me tactfully working it into the conversation.

"It was all a misunderstanding," I said. "I went down to the police station and got it all cleared up."

"That's not what I heard."

So, the cat wasn't just out of the bag; apparently the cat had shredded the bag and managed to fashion it into a clever booby trap.

"What'd you hear?"

"I heard you were hauling drug money and you weren't exactly cooperative during the interview."

I stared at him.

He stared back.

"Who's your source?" I said.

"Doesn't matter. If you're mixed up in anything to do with drugs, I need to know."

The guys over at the computer were pretending not to listen, but they weren't doing a very good job of it.

"There's nothing to know."

"Fine," said Hatch. "When there *is* something, you've got my number."

"Okay, well fine. I just came by to say 'hi' anyway." I got up and started for the door. Hatch didn't budge off the sofa.

"Babe, this stuff can get serious—real quick," he said from across the room. "If you want to talk, I'm off duty tomorrow."

I felt five pairs of eyes follow me out of the day room. I skirted past Mona's desk without saying *aloha* and got into my car. I revved up the engine but didn't put it in gear—just in case Hatch planned to dash out and apologize. After three or four minutes of pretending to warm up the car I shifted into reverse and backed out. Then I popped it into first and laid a little rubber getting out of there.

Next stop, Farrah's.

"You free now?" I said coming in the store from the back alley.

"Well, not exactly free—but I do come cheap." She'd worn that line out ten years ago but I shot her a smile anyway.

"Hey," she went on, "I'm sorry I didn't call you back yesterday. It was wall-to-wall customers all day long and then I had three private tarot sessions last night. But I've been worried about you, so sit down and spill." She pointed to a stool behind the counter and I dragged it over and sat down.

I caught her up on everything that'd happened the past week. When my shop had been next door to Farrah's store we'd never gone more than a day without seeing each other, so it felt weird rehashing stuff that had happened so long ago.

"Okay, let's see if I've got this right: the wedding's off, your red-haired girl's been kidnapped by some low-life druggies, the police are up in your grill about some cocaine money Keith Lewis left you, your kung fu instructor's loser-ass cousin is hiding out at your house, and you just had a squabble with Hatch," she said.

"That's pretty much it in a nutshell," I said.

A guy came in the store to buy a pack of cigarettes and I waited while she rang him up.

"So, about your missing bridesmaid," Farrah said after he left. "Are the police looking for her now that there's a ransom note?"

"I don't know, but it doesn't look like it. Wong made it sound like they think she's just some druggie tourist who got in over her head. He made me promise to stay out of it. I guess they need me to keep quiet so they can turn a blind eye."

"Maybe that's best," she said. "The cops are busy. They don't have the time or money to track down people who are hell-bent on destroying themselves."

"I can't stop thinking about her, though. I found her hair on *my* back seat. Her fingernails were hanging on *my* doorknob, and the ransom note showed up on *my* car. And, no matter how hard I try, I just can't picture the Crystal Wilson I met as some strung-out junkie. She was too *clean*."

"Clean girls get sucked into the life, too, you know. Like all those Hollywood celebrities who've OD'd or graced the cover of *Us* magazine doing the perp walk after getting caught with cocaine at an after-hours club."

"True, but it still feels like something's not right." I picked up a Payday candy bar from the counter display, but when I saw the buck-and-a-half price sticker I put it back down.

"Take it," said Farrah. "It's not like I'm gonna make my best *hoa aloha*—who I hardly ever get to see anymore—pay for a lousy candy bar."

"*Mahalo*," I said. "I'm starving." I tore off the wrapper.

"Oh yeah, and speaking of hardly seeing you anymore," Farrah said over the sound of my munching, "guess what happened next door?"

I shook my head rather than throw out guesses since I was juggling a mouthful of peanuts and caramel.

"Seems they've run into a snag."

I swallowed. "Bad wiring? Rotten wood? What?"

"Well, it all started on Wednesday. I heard yelling and doors slamming and then all kinds of people started traipsing in and out. And not just construction people. There were other people I'd never seen before. The parade kept up all day Thursday. And then this morning, it was quiet—real quiet. Finally, one of the head Mo'olelo guys—I think his name is Tomo or Bobo or something—"

"Bono?"

"Yeah, that's it. Anyway, he comes in around nine to fill his coffee thermos and he gives me an earful." She smiled, apparently enjoying the tale. "Seems they found some wild stuff down in the crawlspace."

"What kind of stuff—like asbestos?"

"Nope, better'n that."

I waited. I've never been a fan of twenty questions but Farrah refused to stop trying to get me to play.

"They found some *iwi*—some bones. From the looks of things they're human—leg bones or arm bones or something. Bono said when they first found them the construction workers shot outta there so fast you'd have thought the place was burning down all over again."

"Did you see them—the bones?" I said.

"Yeah. Bono took me over there and pointed them out. They're right under the floor where they'd torn up some burned-out boards. There are stones there, too—piled up. Everyone agrees it looks like an ancient Hawaiian *heiau*."

"Wow. Like a sacrificial altar or maybe a royal burial spot? Do you think your folks had any idea that was down there when they ran the store?"

"Probably not. But anyway, for now work has stopped—totally *pau hana*. Personally, I think it's pretty funny the historical society got shut down by an inconvenient historical discovery."

"But what about you?" I said. "How do you feel about having ancestor bones right next door?"

"I'm fine with it. Remember, I had a *kahuna* come and bless the store before I opened it back up after the fire. And I'm not afraid of ghosts. Over the years I've bumped into a few ghosts and so far I've gotten along with every one of them. The dead are big on *aloha*."

A smile spread across her face and she went on. "So hey, ol' Bessie Yokamura and her *hupo* Maui Mo'olelo Society thought they could boot you out of your shop and kick you to the curb—no worries. But now they got worries. They can't put a visitor center over sacred ground, and nobody else will want it once they hear about those bones down there. You wait, your phone's gonna start ringing and ol' Bessie's gonna be all happy talking you about how she's changed her mind and she'd *love* to have you as a tenant."

"And I'd love to be back here," I said. "I hate driving to the West Side every day and then trying to get rid of the restaurant smells before my clients show up. If she calls, I'm gonna jump at it, bones or no."

"No, girl. Don't be too quick. *Slippa's* on the other foot now. Doesn't take a psychic to see if you play your cards right you could be paying some dirt cheap rent over there."

We hugged good-bye and I went out to my car feeling pretty good. I could get a *kahuna* to bless my shop and leave the bones to rest in peace. I'd get to work in Pa'ia again, and, if Farrah was right, pay less rent than I had before. Everything was looking pretty good after all.

# 19

I'd like to say Beni Kanekoa cleaned up well, but unfortunately that wasn't the case. His hair was a little less greasy, and he smelled a tad more like soap than scum, but he still resembled something you'd find three-feet down in a Dumpster.

After a few minutes of small talk, Steve, Beni and I ate the rest of our dinner in silence. Steve pushed back from the table and announced he was sorry but he couldn't help with dishes since he'd offered to give a guy a ride somewhere. It was my turn anyway, he didn't need to come up with phony excuses.

After Steve left, I snatched Beni's nearly full plate and scraped it into the garbage. He'd eaten only a few bites, but the alfredo sauce was starting to congeal and I didn't hold out much hope of him suddenly digging in.

"You know, I got the cops after me, too," he said, totally out of the blue. "Seems I got both cops *and* robbers on my tail."

"Beni, hopefully I can help you with the trouble you're in. But first, you're going to have to come clean with me on what you know about Crystal Wilson—you know, the red-haired girl."

"Oh man, that's a freakin' mess. She gets pinched by those guys and then…Hey, I told 'em it was stupid. By the time they figured out I was right, it was a done deal."

"Whoa, wait a minute," I said. "What're you saying? They didn't mean to kidnap her? How do you mistakenly kidnap a person? Doesn't something like that take a lot of planning?"

"I don't know. They don't tell me nothin'. I was only s'posed to make sure that *haole* dude knew they had her. That's all. But then he takes off and it all got fu—uh, I mean, messed up, eh."

"So, why do you think they're coming after you?"

"They gotta blame *somebody*. They finger me for the local dumb-ass so I'll take the fall."

"Okay, let's start at the top. These guys grabbed the red-haired girl when? The day before Halloween?"

"Yeah, the night before. I guess she was at a party at Moose McGillicuddy's down in Lahaina. She left down the back stairs, alone."

"And they abducted her. And then they cut off her hair."

"Yeah, like that."

"And then they told you to make sure Keith Lewis knew about it."

"They called him a different name. But it was the guy you were doing the wedding for," he said.

"The police hinted he'd given me a phony name. Do you remember the name your friends called him?"

"Hey, they're not my friends, eh? They're just some bad-ass dudes I owed a bunch of money."

"Okay, fine. But what name did they call him?" I said.

"Johnson, Jackson, Jock-itch—some stupid *haole* name like that."

"So you're the one who put the hair in my car. Why in my car?"

"Because those guys tol' me to put it where that *haole* guy would find it. But he was staying up at the Ritz. Not like a dude like me can go hangin' around there and not get caught on a camera. I followed him for a while and figured out you were doing his wedding. I remembered you from my cousin's *kung fu* place. On Halloween I follow you to Lahaina and when you park your car I stick it in there. I knew you'd tell him. Smart, eh?"

I chose not to weigh in on his intellectual prowess.

"So, did you also key my car door?"

"Huh? No way, man. The door was open."

Good thing I hadn't perjured myself by agreeing he was intelligent.

"And then when nothing happened after I found the hair," I said, "the kidnappers peeled off her fingernails."

"I s'pose. They don' tell me much."

"So you were the one who hung the bag of fingernails on my doorknob."

"Yeah. I would've put 'em in your car again but I couldn't get in."

"And how about the ransom note?"

"I don't know nothin' about that. After I hung that thing on your door they start accusing me of messing up. They made me point you out. I took 'em by your house and then down to your place in Lahaina. After that, I was pretty out of it." He squirmed in his chair. "Look, we done here? I'm feelin' kind of sick." He belched as if to add authenticity.

"We're done for now. Get some sleep and we'll talk some more in the morning."

"There's nothin' more to say. I did what they told me to do. There's no way this was my idea—no way. Now you gotta help me. I tell ya, if they find me they'll kill me too."

I squinted at him.

He shook his head. "No, I mean it. These dudes have done the deed lots of times—to friends of mine. They squash guys like me like bugs, eh."

Not exactly the note I wanted to end on, but Beni was shaking and sweating like a hosed-down Chihuahua, so I halted my interrogation and helped him get back upstairs to bed.

*\*\*\**

I felt lousy about the way I'd left things with Hatch. I knew I wouldn't be able to get to sleep if I didn't try to straighten things out, so I called him.

"I sure hope you're not calling me from jail," he said as he picked up.

"Very funny. No, I'm here at the house, but I've been feeling bad about how we left things today."

"Bad about being a drug mule, or bad about me finding out about it?"

"Stop it. You know I'm no drug mule. Can I come over and talk?" I didn't want to invite him over to my house and risk having Beni stumble into view.

"I guess. You bringing a peace offering?"

"Sure. You want wine, mac nuts, cookies, what?"

"All of the above, babe. You got some serious making up to do."

I packed a little picnic basket and drove down to Sprecklesville. After my conversation with Beni it felt good to get away from the house for a while. I cranked the driver's side window down and let the trade winds blow my hair around.

I pulled in to Hatch's driveway and slowly approached the house with my headlights off. I was kidding myself if I thought I could sneak up on Wahine, though. Her yapping started when I was still ten yards away, and it changed to a high-pitched whine when I got out of my car. Hatch must have patched the hole in the screen door because she was inside, throwing herself against it in a rather impressive display of righteous indignation.

"Hey, babe," Hatch said as he opened the screen. Wahine shot through the door and off the porch like she'd been launched from a cannon.

"Hey, girl," I leaned down to pet her, but after a quick sniff-assessment of my hand she went for the picnic basket, ignoring my offer of an ear scratching.

"Heen, what have I told you about begging?" said Hatch.

"She probably smells the doggie rawhide I put in there," I said.

"Oh yeah, try and butter up the old man by spoiling his kid." He smiled.

"Seems to be working."

"Not so fast. What've you got in there for me?"

I pulled out a quart of pineapple/mac nut ice cream, some shortbread cookies, and a bottle of white wine.

"Wine and ice cream?" he said.

"Food of the gods."

We sat outside eating ice cream and sipping our wine while Wahine licked and chewed her rawhide. If I hadn't known better, I'd have guessed everything was rosy. A charming little family of three enjoying a night on the lanai while the wind rustled the palms and plumeria blossoms scented the air.

Hatch put his bowl down and Wahine immediately dashed over to lick it clean.

"That's kind of disgusting, you know," I said.

"No, what's disgusting is you getting mixed up with a bunch of scumbag drug dealers."

"That's what I came over to talk about. I—"

"Look, I don't want to hear your excuses. I don't want to hear how all you're doing is trying to find that missing tourist. Fact is, this is quicksand, pure and simple. You watch somebody getting sucked under and you go in to help and the next thing you know, it's you."

I blew out a breath.

"Oh yeah, tell me I don't understand. Call me a hard-ass, or a worry-wart. Thing is—I'm neither. I totally understand. And *not* being a hard-ass nearly killed me."

I waited. There was nothing to say, no question or comment that would make any difference.

"Remember when I told you I left the force over on O'ahu to become a firefighter because I was tired of being a cop—sick of being the dude nobody wanted to see coming? I thought playing fireman would be different. We show up and everybody cheers."

He went on. "Well, come to find out, there's lots of times people want to see cops. Like when I got hit by that jerk while I was working that wreck out on the highway last winter. Nobody cheered louder than me when that cop collared the moron who ran me down."

He paused as if reliving the two months it had taken him to heal from a badly fractured leg and shoulder. And the three months of physical therapy were probably still pretty fresh in his mind as well.

"Anyway, I didn't leave O'ahu willingly—didn't stop being a cop willingly. I left under duress. Under huge freakin' duress."

Wahine lifted her head as if she'd heard a faraway whistle. Then she moved in closer to Hatch and laid her snout on his bare foot. He scratched her head and they both sighed.

"Hatch, I didn't mean—"

"No, let me finish. I haven't told you any of this before because I was hoping I wouldn't have to. Now I know I do."

I gave a small nod, but in the gathering dark I'm not sure he saw it.

"I did the unthinkable—I fell for my female partner. Not supposed to, not encouraged by the department, that's for sure. But we were both single and we understood each other like no one else did. You got someone's back day in and day out and pretty soon you don't have a choice. It's like they become a part of you. In this case, she became the *better* part of me. It wasn't about looks, or sex, or physical chemistry, or any of that. It was about loyalty, and commitment, and not knowing where one of you ends and the other begins."

I felt a tightness grip my sternum. Did I really want to hear his shaggy dog story about his one true love? Hardly.

"Anyway, they tapped her for undercover. She was pretty enough for vice, so I thought they'd be dolling her up and sending her out to Waikiki to nab johns on vacation who chase their mai tais with little blue pills. She couldn't tell me what she was working on, but every night she'd come back a little more tense and a lot more paranoid."

"Finally, I'd had enough," he went on. "On my night off, I tailed her. She didn't go to one of the regular hooker traps, though. She went to a house up in Manoa Valley—way back in there, off the beaten path."

He covered his eyes and then dropped his face into his hands as if watching the memory unspool before him like a movie.

"It turned out to be a drug house—a meth lab. Right after I got there I saw a guy dragging her outside—her arm twisted up behind her back. I panicked, sure her cover had been blown and he'd made her for a cop. I jumped out and as soon as the guy saw me, it was all over. He pulled the biggest damn pistol I've ever seen and blew a huge hole right through her neck. Just like that. I popped him and got her into my car but she bled out before I even hit a paved road."

By now Hatch's voice was a husky whisper. "I didn't go to the memorial service. I didn't even eat for days 'cuz all I wanted to eat was my gun."

Wahine let out a long doggie sigh and nuzzled her snout into the arch of his foot.

"It was my captain's idea for me to switch to the fire service. He had a brother-in-law over here, said he'd let me take the test."

He stopped. Something skittered under the porch but Wahine stayed put.

I had nothing to say—nothing to ask. I laid a hand on Hatch's shoulder.

"Pali," he said. "I'm begging you. Don't get involved in this. Let it go—please."

\*\*\*

It was getting late. On the ride back home I weighed my options but they all came down to one simple truth: I'm not a quitter. I sleep better when I'm not second-guessing myself. Maybe Wong and Hatch were okay with leaving Crystal at the mercy of a bunch of drug-fueled kidnappers, but it wasn't something I could live with.

I came into the house and went upstairs to Beni's room and knocked.

Silence.

"Open the door."

Silence.

"Open this door or I'll break it down."

The sofa bed creaked.

While I waited, I silently counted. When I got to eight, I decided ten was more than he deserved. I took a couple of steps back and heaved my shoulder against the door, but it didn't budge.

Steve jerked his door open at the other end of the hall. "What the hell are you doing?"

"I need to talk to Beni."

"It's after eleven. Let the guy sleep. Besides, he's not going anywhere. You can talk in the morning."

I preferred the visual of crashing through Beni's door and shaking him until his teeth rattled, but common sense won out. After all, I'd be the one paying to fix the door.

I went downstairs and fell on my bed, not even bothering to take off my clothes.

# 20

I'm a light sleeper. I think it comes from being an orphan—I've never felt there was anyone looking out for me but me. So when I sensed someone in my room, I jolted upright. Looking back, I'm pretty sure I smelled him before I actually saw him. This turned out to be a good thing since recognizing his odor was the only thing that kept me from jabbing a knuckle into the larynx of the guy looming over me.

"You awake?" said Beni.

"I am now. What're you doing here?"

"It's not safe up there. I gotta be down here."

"No way, José. In fact, if you ever sneak into my room again, I'll take you out like week-old trash."

"No, listen to me. I showed those guys where you live—re-member? I gotta be where I can take off when they come sniffin' around."

By now I was as awake as I was going to get, so I turned on my bedside lamp. Beni hovered near the end of my bed. He wore a pair of threadbare shorts that hung so low it was pretty obvious he'd blown off my demand to wear underwear. He was bare-chested and his feet were also bare.

"You planning to escape half-naked?" I said.

"I don't need no shoes. They slow me down."

"How about a shirt?"

"Look, I jus' came in here to tell you I'm not staying up-stairs no more. I need to be down here, where I can make a quick getaway without breaking a leg."

"You expect me to trade rooms with you?"

"Nah. I'll sleep on the couch. That way, I can hear 'em coming."

"Fine. But every morning you've got to put away your pillow and blanket—make the room look presentable. I'm not running a flophouse here."

He grunted his agreement and left.

\*\*\*

After Beni's middle-of-the-night foray into my room I slept fitfully until daybreak. I got up at six-thirty and got ready to go down to the PoP to work out some of the anxiety I'd piled on since yesterday—Wong's indifference to Crystal's situation, Hatch's revelation about his past, and Beni's certainty the drug dealers would show up at my door.

By seven I was on my way to the kung fu *guan*, with the rising sun nearly blinding me as I drove down Baldwin Avenue, when my cell phone rang. I checked the caller ID. It read: KINGSTON, O.

"*Aloha*, Ono," I said. "This is Pali. Did you 'butt dial' the wrong number?"

"Hey, what're you talking about? I been waiting for your call. Thought for sure you'd given me the heave-ho."

"Since when is the girl supposed to do the calling?"

"So now you're gonna go all Southern Belle on me? Besides, when we were over in Honolulu you mentioned you were 'kind of involved.' I figured that was a nice way of telling me to shove off."

A few seconds of silence allowed us both time to realize what was going on.

"Okay," I said, "I'm really glad to hear from you. But I'll bet you weren't calling me at the crack of dawn to check on my relationship status. What's up?"

"Tell you what, let me buy you breakfast at Hargrove's. What I've got to say may take a while."

How could I refuse? I loved the mac nut pancakes at Hargrove's, and I only had to walk up thirteen stairs from there to get to my shop. Free breakfast and I didn't have to find a new parking spot—works for me.

"Sounds great, but can you give me a couple of hours? I'm on my way to work out in Pa'ia. I can be down in Lahaina by nine."

"No worries. See you then."

***

Ono looked even better than I remembered. He wore a white cotton shirt with the sleeves rolled up and dark khaki cotton shorts. His tanned face contrasted with his brilliant white smile. I could almost hear Tomika's voice nagging him to get his teeth professionally whitened. *You'll look so good. Ten years younger!* It looked like he'd taken her advice.

We hugged an *aloha* and he asked me what I wanted to eat. I didn't even look at the menu before ordering Kona coffee, guava juice, and mac nut pancakes. If I ever get on death row—which is highly unlikely since Hawaii doesn't allow capital punishment—I'd have no trouble figuring out my last meal. It'd be this very same breakfast.

"You know, today was supposed to be the wedding," said Ono.

"Don't remind me. I've got vendors I've got to pay for *not* using their services. Oh, while I'm thinking of it, how much do I owe you for cancelling?"

"Nothing. Don't worry about it. If I don't take the boat out it doesn't cost me anything."

"How about Tomika? Does she let you just blow off cancellation fees?"

"Ha! You've seen her place. You think she sits up nights tallying up the take on the *Maui Happy Returns?*"

I shrugged. "Well, thanks for that. I'm kind of underwater with this stupid wedding, but I'll manage."

"Anyway, I appreciate you coming down here to meet me," he went on. "I'd probably have dreamed up some excuse to see you again, but when I got wind of this, I had to call."

I was eager to hear what *this* was.

"I guess I should start at the beginning," he went on. "I've already told you my story of how I got to Hawaii and what I'm doing living aboard Tomika's boat."

I nodded.

"But what I didn't clue you in on is what it's actually like living out on the docks. Crazy stuff happens all the time, and I deal with a lot of screwy, scary people—especially after dark."

A different waitress than the one who took our order came by to refill our coffee. Ono shot her his dazzling smile. She gave him a wink and I felt a little put off. Was she trolling for a good tip, or something else?

"Hey, Ono, long time no see," she said in a purring voice that made me think of old Marilyn Monroe movies.

"Hey, Kai, have you met my friend, Pali? She owns a wedding planning shop here in town."

Kai and I smiled and nodded to each other while Ono made the introductions. Then Kai said, "A wedding planner? How fun is that! Too bad I'm already married. I always wanted a big wedding, but Donny wanted to go to Vegas." She shot out a pouty lower lip.

"You could always have a 'renewing of vows' ceremony." I said. "Very popular for ten year anniversaries, and some of them are as fancy as weddings."

She laughed. "Sounds good. That is, if I can manage to stick with Donny for ten whole years. You have no idea what I put up with."

She left and Ono continued. "Anyway, I've nosed around a little and there's dock talk about a suspected kidnapping. Seems the same lowlifes I've locked horns with over drugs are whispering about ransom money for a girl who got nabbed by some serious players."

Even though the waitress had slid a plate of heavenly-scented pancakes in front of me, I didn't look down. Ono had my full attention.

"Drugs are everywhere at the harbor. People hauling 'em, people selling 'em, people getting gutted over a deal gone bad. Just two days after I first brought the catamaran over here a derelict approached me about running 'ice' for him from the Big Island to Maui. Seems they've got a big meth lab over there up in the jungle but distribution's a problem. What with the dogs at the airport, it's tough to bring it in by air."

I could've told him all about the dogs at the airport, but I didn't want to get him off-track.

"Anyway, they're constantly looking for boats to ferry the stuff over. They like day charters, like mine, because if the narcs find drugs aboard you can always blame it on the passengers— say you had no idea it was stashed there, and say you're shocked and horrified to be used like that. With tourism kind of off and on lately, the drug dealers can usually find charter guys who'll haul the stuff when business is slow."

His preamble was going on and on and my pancakes were getting cold. I slathered on butter and doused them in coconut syrup.

"Yum," I said, slicing into the first cake.

"You want me to hold off until you've had a chance to eat?"

"No, go on. I can listen and swoon at the same time."

"So, anyway," he went on, "after keeping this slime at arm's length for a couple of weeks, he decides to change his tactics. I'd been promised a new slip; a great spot, front and center. The harbormaster said the current tenant had given notice and was moving his boat back to the mainland. I put down a deposit and he said the slip would be mine the next weekend. But when the day came to move my boat there was already a big-ass yacht parked in my space. Seems the scuzz ball drug runner had gone to the harbormaster—most likely with either a bribe or a threat—and jerked the slip out from under me. Next thing I know, I'm relegated to Lower Slobovia—way out on the outer docks where I am now."

"Why would a drug runner want a close-in spot? Seems if he's hauling drugs he'd want to keep a low profile."

"Yeah, you'd think, but it wasn't about the slip. It was to put me on notice as to who's really running the harbor. Like a dog peeing on a tree trunk to mark its territory. These guys want everyone out there to know they can act with impunity. *Don't ask, don't tell* may be long gone in the military, but it's alive and well in Lahaina Harbor. And I'm not talking about sexual preferences here."

"Got it. So, tell me about what you overheard about the kidnapping."

"After you called to tell me the bridal couple had taken off and your girl was still missing I did some nosing around. The bottom feeders tend to shoot their mouths off to impress one another. Kidnapping's a Class A felony—big stakes. So, when word came out somebody had grabbed a girl and was holding her for major bucks I put two and two together. I don't have the details, but dollars to doughnuts I'm betting the two things are related. This island's too small for it to be a coincidence. Sounds like a drug deal gone sour."

I cut into my second monster-sized pancake. I'd need to spend an extra sweaty hour in the gym to make up for it, but I didn't care. Not only were the pancakes better than I remembered, but the subject matter made me nervous. I have two ways to deal with stress: either I eat everything in sight, or I don't eat anything for days.

"So," he went on, "does any of this line up with what you've found out about your missing girl?"

"Unfortunately, yes. The cops are playing *see no evil, hear no evil*, but everything I've learned so far points to my sweet-faced bridesmaid being mixed up with local druggies."

"Not much you can do. Probably best to cut her loose."

"I probably should—for a lot of reasons. But I can't. The idea of a young woman coming here to Maui and getting hauled off to who-knows-where by a bunch of scum-sucking drug dealers makes me sick. Okay, maybe she said *yes* when she should've said *no*. Or maybe the partying got a little out of hand. I don't know. But the police aren't the least bit interested. Meanwhile, I'm finding odd body parts on my doorknob and a half-million-dollar ransom note on my car. I've got a convicted felon staying at my house, and I spent half a day getting grilled by the cops for showing up at the airport with cocaine-scented cash."

He put his hand up as if to say, *halt*. "Whoa, whoa. You're getting way ahead of me here."

I filled him in on everything: the fingernails hanging on my shop door when I got back from O'ahu; the ransom note showing up right before Keith and Nicole vanished; the sniffer beagle out at the airport alerting to cocaine on the money Keith left me for the wedding; and finally Beni staying at my house after planting Crystal's hair and nails in my car and at my shop.

"You're probably not safe at your house," Ono said. "Do you want to move down to the boat for a while? I could fix you up a bunk."

"*Mahalo*, but I'm fine. I'm locking my doors, and besides, I'm pretty sure the druggies are done with me. Keith—or whatever his real name is—has most probably gone back to the mainland and Beni's just a small-time hood they used to get to Keith. The way I see it, I'm no longer any use to them."

"Maybe. But you need to get that Beni dude out of your house. He may know more than he's telling. And if he does, they may want to shut him up before he goes running to the cops looking for an immunity deal. You could end up collateral damage."

"But I told you: the cops aren't interested. They've blown me off again and again."

"That doesn't mean squat. Take it from me—cops lie."

By now the waitress had removed our plates and had asked us at least twice if we needed anything more. I looked around. Every table was full. Clearly, we were in jeopardy of overstaying our welcome.

We hugged as we parted. Ono left me with orders to call him after I'd thoroughly debriefed Beni.

I went upstairs to my shop. The message light on my land-line was blinking, but it showed only one message. That was okay, the only person I wanted to hear from was Trish.

# 21

But it wasn't Trish, it was Steve. *Hey Pali, you better get back up here. That stray dog you brought home is tearing the place apart.* In the background I could hear scraping furniture. *Stop it, dude,* yelled Steve. Then the message cut off.

Oh well. I wasn't prepared to explain my situation to Trish anyway, so I hopped in my car and drove back across the island to Hali'imaile. When I came through the back door, everything looked fine in the kitchen. No broken windows, no stuff strewn around or bloody footprints. But as I pushed through the swinging door into the main living area, I stopped. It didn't even resemble my house. The dining table had been upended and shoved up against the picture window that looked out on the street and my six-foot long sofa was blocking the front door. The place looked like it was under siege—like a movie set from *Straw Dogs.*

"What's going on here?" I yelled, even though there was no one around.

Steve came bounding down the stairs. "Looks like your buddy Beni's over his DTs. I'm pretty sure I liked him better when he was messed up."

"Where is he?"

"Don't know. He shoved all this stuff around and then he ducked out back. I tried to stop him and he knocked me into a wall. Check this out." He lifted his arm, displaying a vicious-looking lump on his elbow.

"I'm sorry. We've got to find him. He thinks a bunch of nasty guys are after him."

"Nastier than him? No thanks, I'm staying out of it." He turned to go back upstairs.

"Steve, I need your help. I promise once we find him I'll do the heavy lifting. But right now I could really use another pair of eyes looking for him."

He smacked the banister. "Is that all I am to you? Another pair of eyes?"

I stared him down—literally.

We got outside and I directed Steve to go left while I went right. The detached garage was on my side, so I quietly pulled the man door open and peered inside. Steve's immaculate black Jetta was parked squarely in the middle of the space. The tidy shelves he'd built for me lined the walls on either side, and there were cardboard boxes stacked three high on each shelf.

"Beni? It's me, Pali. Are you in here?"

Only the sound of the wind whistling through the cracks in the old plank walls disturbed the silence.

"Beni, if you're in here, please say something. I believe you about those guys being after you. We need to find you a better place to hide."

There was a *click* and the passenger door of Steve's car opened a crack. The interior light blinked on, and then the door quickly closed again. I went over to that side of the car.

"Beni, come out. I'm serious. I don't think it's safe for you here. If you'll come out and talk with me, I promise I'll try and find you a better hiding place."

By now Steve must have heard me, because he was standing in the doorway of the garage.

"Is he in my car?" he shrieked. "Oh my god. I've got the King of Stink undoing two years of carefully maintaining that new car smell. Of all my five senses, olfactory's my favorite! Get him out of there."

I opened the passenger door, and found Beni huddled on the floorboard between the seat and the dashboard. He was folded in thirds, which made him look about six years old. When he turned his face to me, there were tear tracks down his cheeks.

"Beni, did something happen?"

He nodded.

"What?"

"I remembered."

"We need to get back in the house. Steve will watch and make sure nobody's coming. You're going to tell me everything, and then we'll find you a safer place to hide. Okay?"

"No, I like it here in the car."

"Beni, we don't have time for this. If you don't come out right now, I'm going to pull your ass out. And, don't worry, I'm more than capable—just ask your cousin Doug."

I reached in to grab him but he unfolded his arms and hoisted himself up onto the seat before I could get a firm grip.

As soon as Beni was upright and out of the car, Steve rushed over to survey the damage.

"Leave it," I said. "We'll open all the doors and let it air out. I need you to keep watch at the house while I grill Beni about what he remembers."

Steve made a grunting noise—not agreeing, but not disagreeing either.

I popped the car doors open while Beni slinked toward the outside door. He waited for me to join him before venturing outside.

"You got a gun?" he said.

"No, but I've trained with your cousin for seven years now. I've got a couple of black belts and I've kicked major ass in a ton of tournaments."

He snorted. "Big whoop. What you gonna do, karate chop a bullet coming at me?"

"Get in the house, Beni. The quicker you start talking, the quicker I'm gonna begin caring about what happens to you."

\*\*\*

Beni insisted we talk in my bedroom. He said he thought it was safer in there, with the window shades down and Steve standing sentry at the front door.

"Okay, dude," I said. "I need to know everything."

"Can you get me something to eat? I'm real hungry."

"First you talk, then you eat. I doubt if the cockroaches holding Crystal Wilson are ringing up room service every time her stomach growls."

He mumbled something I couldn't make out.

"What'd you say?"

"Nothin'."

"Beni, I'm totally serious. Talk—now."

"Okay." He picked at the chenille tufts on my bedspread.

I waited.

"From the get-go it was this guy named Slam's idea. Seems he got a call from some honcho on the mainland. The way he told it, this mainland guy had a beef with your wedding dude. So Slam comes up with the idea of snatching one of the girls from your guy's wedding and making him pay a big ransom to get her back. After he picked her up, he cut off her hair and had me put it in your car, like I tol' you before."

"Did he tell you to put it in my car? I thought you dreamed that up on your own."

"Nah, you're right. He said to make sure the guy saw it. I told him you were doing the guy's wedding and I knew you'd tell him 'bout it. Then when Slam didn't hear nothing from that Jackson dude, he took off her fingernails. He said that's the kind of stuff his boss does on the mainland—you know, take body parts. Anyway, he wanted Jackson to know he had the girl and he was *da kine* serious."

"Beni, you're plowing old ground here. Get to the part about what you remembered just now."

"When Slam didn't hear back nothin' from the fingernails, he got *beef*—you know, what *haoles* call 'pissed off'. He call me up and said I messed up. Said we weren't square and if I wanna get square I gotta do one more job."

He'd picked an entire tuft of chenille off my bedspread. I was itching to slap his hand and tell him to knock it off, but I didn't want to stop the story.

"So anyway, I went up there where he was and he—"

"Wait a minute, where was he?"

"Up at 'Iao Valley. Way past the parking lot, up on the hill. He musta been some kind of Boy Scout or somethin' cuz he was running all kinda crazy up through there, jumpin' over rocks and bushes and stuff. It was *pa'akiki* keeping up with that dude."

Another tuft of chenille bit the dust.

"So anyways, we get way up in there, and he's got this girl in a blue tent. She had hardly any hair on her head, but she was still a looker. They had her all tied up. She wasn't freaking out or nothin', though. I gotta say, either she was real doped up and or she didn't realize what was going down. She wasn't screaming or cryin'—nothin' like that. She just sat there, watching us. Never once made a sound." He stared down at the bare spots he'd made on my bedspread.

I waited. After a half-minute of silence, I nudged him on. "So, what'd you do?"

"Whaddaya mean? What'd *I* do? I followed orders, man. When that Jackson dude took off and didn't give them their money Slam got real pissed off. But I didn't have nothin' to do with snatchin' that girl or any of that."

"Okay, so why do you think the police are after you? Seems to me if you'd tell them what you know about this kidnapping, you'd be a hero."

"Jeez, are you stupid? It's not like that. They're gunnin' for me."

"Are you saying the police might be somehow involved in it?"

"Well, duh. Give the lady a prize." He snorted and leaped up from the bed. "I need a lawyer, man. No offense or nothin', but you're lame. I need to get off this rock, maybe go over to Kauai and see some friends I got there. Lay low for a while. But first I gotta find me a lawyer who can cut a deal with the cops."

\*\*\*

When I pulled in behind the Palace of Pain, Sifu Doug's Jeep was the only car in the alley. So far, so good. I just needed three minutes of one-on-one time.

I went inside and he was in the far corner, sitting cross-legged on the mat, apparently deep in meditation. Under normal circumstances, I'd have tip-toed to the changing room and quietly put on my uniform. Unfortunately for me, normal circumstances had gone AWOL ten days ago.

"Sifu? Sorry to interrupt, but I need to talk to you."

He opened one eye and gave me the look I'm sure cinched him getting picked for Special Forces a decade earlier. "I was meditating. You know the rules."

"Yes, and I know the punishment, but this can't wait, Sifu. It's about your cousin."

He shot me a wry smile.

"He's in huge trouble," I went on, "and not just with those drug dealers. Now he thinks the police are after him too."

"Pali, the dude's done hard time. He's a drug user and a well-known dealer. I can't think of a time when the cops *weren't* after him."

"No, this time it's different. He's scared and he wants to turn himself in, but he's convinced the police are involved in Crystal's disappearance. He wants someone to go talk to them on his behalf. I thought about your brother James, the lawyer. He did a good job for us last time. Do you think you could put in a good word and see if he'll help Beni?"

"You know how many times James has pulled Beni's sorry butt outta the fire? Ten, maybe twelve times now. James is getting a rep down at the courthouse for doing more *pro bono* work for his dumb-ass cousin than he does for actual paying clients."

I gave him my *I'm begging you* face.

"Okay, okay. I'll call James and see what he says. But he's not gonna be happy about it."

"Tell him it's an emergency. Beni's got solid information on a kidnapping that he's willing to trade for leniency and safe passage to Kauai. He's gone up to where they're holding my missing girl, Crystal Wilson. She's up in 'Iao Valley. If we move fast enough we can probably find her."

Doug shook his head. "She's been gone for what—ten days—now? I think you better prepare yourself for a worst case scenario, Pali."

"You, of all people, are telling me to give up?"

"Look, you grew up here, but your auntie sheltered you from the kind of scum Beni hangs out with. I've seen what those bottom feeders will do for a snort or a hit. And I'm sorry to say, but I got a bad vibe about your missing girl's chances."

"But you'll call James?"

"It's a done deal, Pali."

I bowed deeply from the waist. "*Mahalo,* Sifu. And with all due respect, I think you're wrong about Crystal. Beni said she was acting very calm—not trying to escape or give the kidnappers any grief. I'm hoping that now they know the ransom isn't going to get paid they'll just abandon her. But she won't last long up there in that valley all by herself. We need to get moving."

# 22

I stopped by Farrah's on my way home from Palace of Pain. She was in the store, dusting bottles of expensive balsamic vinegar that'd been there for months and would probably never find a home. In traditional Hawaiian-style cooking we use a lot more Spam than prosciutto, and we go heavy on the mayo, but pass up the extra virgin olive oil.

"Hey," Farrah said, "must be my lucky day—seeing you two days in a row."

"I was down at the PoP. Thought I'd drop by before going home."

"And...?" She cocked her head.

"And, I'm kind of at loose ends."

"Still worried about your girl?"

"More than ever."

I told her about my breakfast meeting with Ono and Beni's recent recollection of having gone to the kidnapping site.

"Do you believe him?" she said.

"Yes and no."

"Meaning..."

"Meaning it seems like he knows a heckuva lot more than he's telling me. But I can't push him too hard. He's drying out from a drug binge and he's paranoid."

"What about?"

"He doesn't think he's safe up at my place," I said. "And truthfully, I won't be sorry to see him leave. But I haven't a clue where to stash him until his lawyer can work out a deal with the police."

"Why don't you bring him down here?" By now she'd moved from dusting stock to standing behind the sales counter. She opened the cash drawer and took out a fistful of coins and started stacking them into coin wrappers.

"Farrah, the whole town comes through here. According to him, he's got a target on his back and probably a price on his head. Half an hour after someone sees him here, one of your customers will blab to his sister, who'll turn around and tell her neighbor. Then the neighbor will call his cousin who's either a cop or a drug dealer. Whichever way it goes down, it's not a happy outcome for Beni."

"I wouldn't have him stay down here in the store. I'd put him in my apartment—upstairs. Nobody but you knows I'm up there. He'd be totally off the radar."

I hesitated. The last thing I wanted was to drag my best friend into what was quickly becoming a complicated—and risky—mess.

"Besides," she went on, "you said yourself you don't think he's being straight with you. I've got ways to make him talk."

Unlike me, Farrah doesn't rely on physical strength to subdue her opponents. With her it's strictly mental. She's skilled at using paranormal, psychological, and her self-described 'womanly wiles' to get people to do what she wants. And once she's made up her mind about something—game over.

"Okay, I'll bring him down. You really think you can get him to tell all?"

She pulled a ten-dollar bill from the till. "I got a handsome dead president here who says I can."

"I'm not betting with you. I can't afford to lose—again."

"Okay, no money—just bragging rights. Give me an hour or so, then bring him down—after one-thirty. It doesn't look like I'm gonna have much of a lunch rush today, but just in case, let's hold off until I'm sure I'll have plenty of time to get our pal Beni settled in."

\*\*\*

When I told Beni the news he scowled. "I know her. She's that hippie chick who runs the Pa'ia store. That place charges like double what you'd pay for a pack of smokes at WalMart."

"Doesn't matter. She won't let you smoke there anyway."

"I'm not going."

"Your choice. But if you stay here I'm calling Detective Wong at the Police Department and tell him how you and your buddy Slam kidnapped Crystal Wilson and took her up to 'Iao Valley. He's got the ransom note so he'll be eager to see who wrote it."

"I told you—I didn't kidnap her. I just planted the hair and stuff."

"Doesn't matter. What you did is called being an 'accessory to a crime.' And guess what? It carries the same punishment as the crime. And the crime we're talking about here—kidnapping with intent to extort a ransom—is a Class A felony. Conviction means twenty years hard time."

He sneered as if I'd just told him a really old, really feeble, joke.

I went on. "And, thanks to you, now I'm in the same boat. Since I'm harboring a fugitive involved in a major felony, I could be accused of obstruction of justice. They can go for hard time on that one too, but if I give you up to the cops, I'll probably walk."

"I told you to *get* me a lawyer, not *talk* like one."

"Okay, I already did that. I asked Sifu Doug to call your cousin, James, and see if he's willing to help."

Beni shook his head. "That dude's weak, man. I been to court with him like a million times and every single time I end up in jail. He's so lame he couldn't keep his own self out of jail if the judge was his mama."

"Beni, you're a convicted drug dealer. I don't think Gloria Allred's gonna be flying in anytime soon to defend your bony ass."

"Who?"

"Listen, Farrah's offered to hide you in her apartment until you and James can work something out with the police. Take it or leave it."

"It true she won't let me smoke at her place? Not even regular cigarettes?"

"We leave in about an hour. I suggest you use the time to take a shower."

\*\*\*

Farrah greeted Beni with a warm hug, which was pretty darn big of her since Beni hadn't used his time to take a shower but instead had paced the backyard sucking down cigarettes as fast as he could light them. My car, my hair, my entire *body* reeked of burned tobacco—but it was nothing compared to the cloud of funk coming off Beni.

"*Ho'okipa* to my home, *Peni'amina*," Farrah said as she stepped back to survey the skinny, disheveled man standing before her.

"Huh?" said Beni.

"*Ho'okipa* means welcome."

"I know that," he snarled. "What's that other thing you said?"

"*Peni'amina?* That's your name—Benjamin—in Hawaiian. I looked it up."

"The name's Beni. Just Beni. Nobody—not even my dead *tutu*—ever called me Benjamin."

Farrah locked eyes on mine. Her face revealed she was none too pleased with her new guest. She looked as if she'd been promised winsome George Clooney and "winning" Charlie Sheen had shown up instead.

I glanced around the tiny apartment. "Well, I'll let you two work out the sleeping arrangements. I need to get back down to Palace of Pain and pick up James. He doesn't want anyone to see him coming or going. Doesn't want to tip off anyone looking for Beni."

"Ha! What he don't want," Beni said, "is to get the window in his fancy Mercedes busted out, like last time. The guy's *hupo*—stupid. He got no street smarts. When I get a chance I'm gonna find me a better lawyer—an *akamai* one with enough brains to bribe the judge. I'm sicka doin' time 'cuz that dude's a Twinkie."

"Twinkie?" said Farrah.

"Yeah, you know, like brown on the outside but white and squishy on the inside."

I hurried down the stairs. The faster a deal could be worked out with the police, the faster Beni'd be gone and my best friend could get someone to fumigate her apartment.

***

The blinds were drawn in Sifu Doug's office. I heard James and Doug talking in low tones but they stopped as soon as I rapped on the office door.

"Who goes there?" said Sifu Doug in his Army Ranger voice.

"It's me—Pali."

"Enter."

I'd seen James before, under both social and professional circumstances, but he looked different this time. His face looked pale and pinched; his eyes merely slits. He was perched on the edge of a folding chair, wearing a black and tan aloha shirt and khaki pants. A beige sport coat was draped over the back of his chair. He stood when I entered.

"James," I said, extending my hand.

"Hey Pali." He gave me a half-hearted handshake.

"C'mon, *brudda*," Doug said, sounding as if he was picking up their conversation from where they'd left off. "He's family. And it's not like it's you who's going to jail."

"Dealing with him is worse than jail. Beni serves his time and it's over. For me, it's a never-ending string of insults and snide remarks. He's trashed my reputation. Even the judges take shots at me 'cuz I sound like a fool trying to defend him."

"I got that, but you know Mom would freak out if you refused. No way she's gonna allow her sister's baby boy to use a public defender when we've got a lawyer in the family."

James turned to me. "He's up at your place?"

"No, he moved. He didn't think it was safe at my house, so I found him new digs."

"You gonna tell me what's going on here?" said Sifu Doug.

"It's best if you don't know any more than you do," said James.

James and I went outside and he pulled a briefcase from the trunk of his midnight blue Mercedes sedan.

"Gorgeous car," I said.

"Yeah, well, there's the good news and the bad news with this ride. Everybody sees it and thinks I'm doing great. But the truth is, I'm working fifty to sixty hours a week to keep up the payments. And all this *pro bono* crap with Beni sure doesn't help."

We went over to my sad-looking car and James got in without comment. I pulled out of the alley and headed up Baldwin Avenue.

"The state doesn't pay you to defend guys like Beni?"

"I'd get a small fee if the case was assigned to me by the court. But when you do it on your own—like this, with my family putting the screws to me—then it's totally on my dime. I've even got to foot the bill for expenses."

"Well, I'm sure Beni appreciates it."

He laughed. "Hardly. He's the worst client possible. I bust my butt getting through law school and passing the bar exam and I'm rewarded with a blood-sucking dipshit of a cousin as my number one client. He's never paid me a dime—or even given me so much as a *mahalo* for my effort."

I pulled into the alley behind Farrah's store and parked.

"He's here? At the Pa'ia Store?" said James. "Not a very smart hiding place."

"He's upstairs."

"I didn't know there was an upstairs."

"Exactly."

I checked to make sure there was no one in the alley before we got out. We went up the back stairs and I used my special knock to let Farrah know it was me. When she opened up, she looked liked she'd been sucking on a lemon and a seed had gotten stuck in her throat.

"Way glad to see you," she said.

"Where's Beni?" said James, looking around the cramped living room.

"He's barricaded himself in my bathroom. I even had to go downstairs to pee." She pointed toward her bedroom. "It's through there."

James went into the bedroom and a few seconds later I heard him tapping on the bathroom door announcing his arrival.

"How're you doing?" I said to Farrah.

"You should've warned me."

"I tried. But he'll only be here a day or two at the most. I've alerted James that time is of the essence if we hope to find Crystal in decent shape. After ten days the poor girl's probably wondering if anyone's even looking for her."

Farrah shot me a look.

"What?" I said.

"Pali, you're a good person. But these people aren't. Don't get your hopes up."

"Sheesh, what's with everybody? First Sifu Doug goes all gloom and doom on me and now you? We need to get moving, but since we know where she is, we should be able to find her pretty fast."

"From your lips to God's ear," she said. "But, as you said before, chances are Beni hasn't told us everything."

# 23

That night, as Steve and I were eating dinner, the phone rang. He got up and checked the caller ID. "It's Farrah," he said, handing me the receiver.

"Hi," I said. "What's up?"

"Can you come down here?"

"I'm in the middle of dinner. How 'bout giving me half an hour?"

"Pali, I wouldn't ask if it wasn't important. Please, get down here as soon as you can."

"What's going on? Are you okay?"

"Just get down here." She hung up.

As I headed for the back door I asked Steve to stick my plate in the oven. "I'll be back in a little while to finish it."

"Everything okay?" he said.

"Apparently not."

The trip down Baldwin Avenue seemed to take forever. What had Beni done now? The guy was smelly, rude, and infuriating, but Farrah had infinite patience. I was speeding ten miles over the limit and yet it felt like my wheels were slogging through mud.

Farrah opened her apartment door. "Come in."

I looked around her dimly lit living room. Beni was nowhere in sight.

"Did your new roommate take off?" I said.

"I wish. He's holed up in the john again."

"So, what's going on?"

She gestured toward her lumpy sofa. "Sit. You need to hear this sitting down."

As soon as I sat,' Farrah's Jack Russell terrier, Sir Lipton, jumped in my lap. The dog had been named before her gender had been correctly determined, so her name should've been Lady Lipton, but Farrah refused to acknowledge the error.

"Lipton's such a good boy. He always knows when to lend support," she said.

"Okay, spill," I said. "The suspense is killing me."

"Oh, Pali. I know you've been really concerned about that bridesmaid. You know, Crystal Wilson."

She paused. I waited. That kind of phony tee-up from Farrah almost always signaled disaster.

"I'm afraid the news isn't good. A little while ago Beni told me those druggies he's hiding from killed her."

My thinking slowed way down. I couldn't even form a complete sentence. "What? Why?"

"I guess when they sent Keith the ransom note and he just took off, they went nuts. They blamed Beni and made him watch while they killed her."

"Beni's not the most reliable source of information, you know."

"Yeah, but I believe him. He was there—he saw stuff. I called you down here to break the bad news myself, before he goes to the cops."

"As if the cops give a damn," I said.

"So, what now?"

"I don't know. Give me a minute."

The anger that erupted in me came as a surprise. Farrah snatched Lipton from my lap just in time to avoid the poor dog getting dumped on the floor.

"Those bastards!"

I felt something rattling around the back of my mind but I couldn't put my finger on it. I started pacing.

"I'm so sorry, Pali. I wish I didn't have to tell you this. You and I aren't strangers to heartbreak, that's for sure." Farrah and I had both been orphaned when we were young, and she'd recently had to deal with the death of a newfound love interest.

"I can't even imagine how horrible this was for her," I said. "All alone, so young and far from home. Being held by a bunch of drug-crazed assholes who chopped off her hair and ripped off her fingernails. She must have been terrified."

"If it's any consolation, Beni said she was incredibly brave, right up to the end."

"Sorry, but that's no consolation. In fact, it makes me even more pissed off." I slammed my fist into my palm. "Would you get Beni out here? I need to talk to him."

"He probably won't come, he's afraid. He said his cousin Doug told him you could kick his ass from here to Hana, and he's scared you're gonna do it."

"I'd like nothing better, but I promise to maintain control. Please go get him."

Beni hung his head as Farrah led him into the room. "Sorry, man," he said.

"Sorry? You let them kill a defenseless woman in cold blood and you think you can wipe it away with a 'sorry'? How screwed up are you? I tried to help you. I even worried about you." By now I was in full shriek mode.

"No, man. Listen. I didn't do nothin'. They said they'd send their guys after me if I didn't show. So I go up there. They were way deep up in there, man. They give me a *da kine* shovel and say dig a big hole. I figured they were messing with me but then I get they're serious. It takes me a long time to dig the hole, and when I get done I go down to where they were in this blue tent. I see that girl—with the hair chopped off. Next thing I know they drag her out. They push her, like down on her knees."

He hung his head.

"And then what, Beni?"

"I didn't wanna look. She didn't scream or beg or nothin'. And then Slam pulls a gun and there were two shots—*bam! bam!*"

"You didn't try to stop him? You just let him murder this poor girl right in front of you?"

"I didn't know. I didn't..." He put his hands over his face.

"So then what'd you do?"

"Whaddaya think? I took off runnin'."

"Did you think he'd shoot you too?"

"Hell, yeah. Those dudes don't want no witness. And that hole I dug was plenty big for two."

It was hard for me to feel sorry for Beni, but I did. How did the sweet little fifth-grader I'd met ten years earlier at Sifu Doug's manage to grow up to be such a degenerate *'okole*?

At that moment I recalled what had been rattling around the back of my mind: Hatch's fiancée. She'd been murdered the same way—executed by drug dealers. Hatch went into a steep nosedive after witnessing her murder. And now it'd happened again. I was used to watching nightly reports on the Honolulu news detailing crimes committed by O'ahu drug lords. But Honolulu was a big city; drugs and crime came with the territory. Over there it was expected, but here on Maui it was a disgrace.

"Beni, I know a sure-fire way to get the police to offer you protection," I said.

"Yeah?"

"First light tomorrow, you and I are going to retrace your trip up to 'Iao Valley. We're going to find that hole you dug and take some pictures. The Maui cops will have to take us seriously or we'll let them know we'll go over their heads."

"But what if Slam and those other dudes are still up there?"

"What're the chances of that?" I didn't wait for him to answer before saying. "Zero. Why would those scum bags hang around a murder scene out in the middle of nowhere?"

He shrugged.

"I know it's a little scary, but it's the only way. We'll go up there and get evidence. The police will have to act. You with me on this?"

He gave me a nearly imperceptible nod.

"Good. I'll pick you up around six. The sun will be coming up by then but the park won't be open yet."

I gave Farrah a hug and went back down to my car.

On my way home in the dark, the boogey man began whispering in my ear. Why had Crystal's disappearance gone unnoticed? Why had there been no news reports of her kidnapping, or requests for the public to keep an eye out for her? There'd apparently been no calls from family or friends inquiring about her whereabouts—or if there had been, they'd been ignored. Could the Maui Visitor's Bureau have so much clout they could squelch news that cast our idyllic island in a bad light? Or was Beni correct in accusing the police of collusion? Whatever the reason, it seemed pretty clear if we didn't make some noise, Crystal Wilson's murder would disappear—like footprints swept away by the tide.

Not on my watch. If Glen Wong wanted to throw me in jail for doing the job he refused to do, then so be it. He could argue that Crystal's death was simply a bad end for a mainland party girl who'd gotten herself tangled up with local dope peddlers, but I didn't buy it. A young woman—a human being—had been executed, supposedly collateral damage in a beef between a couple of lowlife drug dealers. She'd been buried in the loamy soil of the rain forest where the daily downpours and warm temperatures would quickly reclaim her body to the earth. We had to find her. Her soul deserved to rest in peace knowing the lowlifes who'd brutally ended her short life had been brought to justice.

Game on, scumbags.

# 24

When I got back home I was in no mood to eat the dinner waiting for me in the oven. I scraped it into the garbage and was rinsing my plate when Steve came into the kitchen.

"Everything okay?" he said.

"Not by a long shot."

He waited while I stuck the plate in the dishwasher and slammed the door shut.

"Got it. You're mad. What's the deal? Beni come up with yet one more way to piss you off?"

I couldn't help it—I started to cry.

"Hey, hey," he said. "The guy's a dipshit. Don't give him the satisfaction."

"No, it's not about Beni," I said. "Well, it's kind of about him, but not totally."

Steve squinted his eyes in confusion and then reached into his pocket for a freshly pressed hankerchief. He's the only guy I've ever met who still carries cotton handkerchiefs. He handed it to me and I wiped my nose.

"Sorry for the waterworks," I said.

"Hey, you've had a lousy week."

"Not as lousy as some people. I gotta sit down," I said. I sat at the kitchen table and Steve took the chair across from me. "Beni says those drug dealers killed Crystal Wilson." I filled Steve in on the few facts I'd gleaned from Beni—that he'd been ordered to dig a hole up in 'Iao Valley; that he'd seen Slam shoot Crystal in the head; and that after the shooting he'd run away.

"Wow. Do you believe him? You've got to call Glen Wong with this."

"Yes, I believe him, and no, I'm not calling Wong."

Steve sat tight, staring me into continuing.

"I believe Beni witnessed the murder," I said. "That's why he's so freaked about those guys coming after him. And the reason I'm not calling Wong is because when I gave him the ransom note he made me promise I'd leave it all up to them."

"I doubt he ever imagined you'd be hanging out with an eyewitness to murder," Steve said. "Things have changed."

"No, you don't understand. He was adamant about keeping this a police matter. He made it quite clear he wanted me to butt out."

"Well, how about *I* call Glen? I could tell him I overheard something. He knows how much the guys at the bar blab after a couple of martoonies." Steve and Glen Wong traveled in the same social circle—although Steve was way out of the closet while Detective Glen Wong was back in there so far you couldn't have found him with a flashlight.

I didn't want to tell Steve about Beni's assertion that the police were dirty, and maybe even complicit. First, because Beni'd been on the wrong side of the law for so long he wasn't the best judge of character, and second, because Wong was a friend of Steve's and I didn't want to throw Steve into a moral dilemma about whether or not he should tip off Wong.

"I don't know," I said. "These drug dealers are dangerous. If word ever got out you were the snitch, they'd probably come gunning for you. And then I'd have to break in a new roommate, and remember to take fresh flowers up to your grave every week, and—"

"Okay, okay. So, what're you gonna do?"

"I'm going to go up there and find some convincing evidence. The only way Wong's going to take me seriously is if I bring him something he can't sweep under the rug, like he did with the hair and the ransom note. Think about it—I go to him with some tale I heard from a convicted meth dealer? I mean, really, if I were Wong, I probably wouldn't believe any of this either."

"But *you* do—believe Beni, that is."

"I'm afraid so," I said.

"So how're you going to get this so-called 'convincing evidence'?"

"I'm going up to 'Iao Valley tomorrow morning and find the campsite where Beni dug Crystal's grave."

"You're gonna just tromp right into a drug nest up in the wilds of 'Iao Valley? Wait a sec, let me look up the number for the suicide hotline. I'm sure they'd like to weigh in on this. And besides, there's like a zillion acres of rain forest up there. How'll you even know where to start?"

"I didn't say I was going by myself."

***

When Farrah opened the door to her apartment the next morning, she informed me that Beni was once again holed up in the bathroom.

"I yelled at him that you were on your way up, but he didn't come out," she said.

I went to the bathroom and rapped on the door. "Get out here, Beni. It's time for our 'Iao Valley field trip."

No response.

"Or, if you'd rather, we could take a short drive over to the Wailuku Police Station and tour that instead."

Again, no sound.

"You know I'm not above breaking down this door."

Not so much as a whimper.

"You have a key for this?" I asked Farrah.

"No, but look at it. It's just a crummy *puka* lock," she said. "I'll bet I can get it open with a bobby pin." She rummaged around in her nightstand and came up with a pin. She dug around in the lock for about ten seconds and then the bolt clicked as it cleared the latch.

Farrah's bathroom was so tiny it didn't take long to figure out it was unoccupied. In fact, the only evidence that Beni'd been hanging out in there for hours on end was a lingering malodorous tang in the air.

"How'd he get out?" I asked.

"Heck if I know," Farrah said. "That little window opens onto the roof. From there he'd have to climb across the roof and then drop down almost eight feet to the eaves on the first floor. It's another ten feet down to the alley."

"It could be done," I said.

"By your Sifu Doug, maybe. But Beni? The guy had trouble buttering a piece of bread."

"Desperate times require desperate measures," I said.

"So now what?" she said.

I gave her my most soulful stare.

"No. No way. I can't go up there with you. You know how sensitive my psyche is to stuff like they got going on up there."

Farrah wasn't talking about possibly running into the drug dealers, or even being squeamish about finding Crystal Wilson's body. I'd known her long enough to know she was referring to the bloody history of the 'Iao Valley. In 1790, Kamehameha the Great came over from the Big Island of Hawaii to lay claim to Maui. He killed Maui's head chief and forced the Maui warriors deeper and deeper into 'Iao Valley before unleashing fire from a cannon he'd seized from a *haole* ship. The Maui fighters never had a chance. The bloodshed was so horrendous they named the battle *Kapaniwai*, or "the damming of the waters" because piles of dead warriors' bodies clogged 'Iao Stream, reducing it to a trickle. The little water that did get through ran blood red. For more than a century no one ventured into the valley. The screams and moans of the ghosts trapped there could be heard for miles around.

"You want me to go up there all by myself?"

"No, I think you should call Hatch, or maybe the cops."

Neither of those options appealed to me.

"I'll tell you what. I'll ask Ono to go with me. You stay here and call me if Beni shows up. As much as I'd like to never deal with that scum sucker again, it'd make it much easier to find Crystal if I had some idea of where to start looking."

"Oh. I almost forgot," Farrah said. "Beni said something last night that sounded kind of feeble at the time, but it might help: he said they went alongside the stream from where it goes through the park. Once they started climbing, he got worried about finding his way back. He began singing "Ninety-nine Bottles of Beer on a Wall" in his head so he'd be able to figure out how far he'd gone. He was at thirteen bottles of beer when they finally got to the campsite."

"Really? Mr. Mope-a-dope had the presence of mind to sing eighty-six stanzas of a stupid drinking song while he hiked up the valley? Maybe his whole strung-out act is just that—an act."

"Hard to say. But he sang a little of it for me. And he sang it pretty slow. Like this: 'Ninety-nine...bottles of...beer...on the wall…' Like that. So, hopefully that gives you some kind of idea as to how far up he went."

I gave her a hug and left. On my way down to the car I called Ono.

"Hey, two calls in two days," he said when he picked up the call. "I'm flattered. Howzit shakin'?"

I quickly filled him in on what I'd learned over the last two days about Crystal Wilson's fate. When Ono responded, his voice was two octaves lower.

"Those rotten sons of bitches," he said. "I had a bad feeling about this from the get-go. What can I do?"

"Can you go up to 'Iao Valley with me this morning? I'd rather not go up there alone."

"I'd rather you not go up there at all. This is some serious shit, Pali. I think you should call the cops and let them handle it."

"I plan on calling them, after I verify Beni's story. He's not the most reliable source, and I'm afraid they'll blow me off again if I don't bring them something to prove Crystal's been murdered."

"Don't you think you should at least give them a heads up on what you've heard?"

"No, I don't. I don't want to go into it now, but I don't want to give them any more information until it's absolutely necessary. So, how about it—are you up for a little stroll in the woods with me?"

"Sure, I'll come. But I'll be loaded for bear. Last thing I need is to be ducking through the underbrush trying to dodge some strung-out druggie taking pot shots at us."

"You've got a gun?"

"I didn't say that. And it's best I don't say anything. What you don't know can't be held against you. When are you thinking of going?"

"Right away. I'd like to get up there before too many tourists show up."

"Tell you what. Can you give me a couple of hours? I've got an idea and I'll need that much time to run down the details."

"Okay, let's meet there at eight-thirty. I'll park on the road, just outside the pay parking lot."

"See you there," he said, and signed off.

\*\*\*

I drove out Highway 32 through Wailuku to the entrance to 'Iao Valley with my stomach twisted into a tight knot. I dreaded seeing Crystal's fresh grave—or worse. What if they hadn't bothered to bury her after Beni fled the scene? I pride myself on being tough physically, but emotionally I'm a lightweight. Even though I have no qualms about laying an opponent out flat as a stingray in a martial arts fight, I don't deal well with everyday grief and gore. And I'd never seen a dead body outside of a coffin. What if I threw up—or fainted? I'd watched enough cop shows to know rookie homicide detectives usually toss their lunch the first time they process a murder scene.

No use kidding myself. The next few hours weren't gonna be pretty.

# 25

I parked on the side of the road just outside the marked entrance to 'Iao Valley State Park. Only tourists pay the five bucks they demand for parking inside the lot, and besides, it was still early and the road was empty.

I was chiding myself for rushing up here just so I could sit around for an hour waiting for Ono when my cell phone rang. The caller ID said, *Powell, Patricia*. I didn't know anyone by that name, but I answered anyway.

"Hi Pali. It's me, Trish. You out of jail yet?"

"Hi Trish. No, I never was in jail. It was just a huge misunderstanding."

"How come you never called me back?"

"I did call you. I figured you hadn't returned my call because you were busy with your conference."

There was a long pause. "I called you back," she said. "You owed me a call, I'm sure of it."

I could see how this was playing out, so I let her win.

"My bad. What's on your mind?"

"I'm thinking of coming back over to Maui. You think you can pick me up without getting arrested this time?" She said it with a chuckle, but it sounded more like a taunt.

"When are you coming? Today's Sunday, and I don't usually work on Sundays."

"Well, this is my last day in Hawaii, so it's now or never."

"Trish, I'm so sorry, but I can't possibly meet with you today."

"What? Are you kidding? I came all the way over here just to see you. I even lied to my boss and everything." I heard her suck in a quick breath before she continued. "Oh, I get it. You're blowing me off. You don't want to do my wedding. It's against the law to discriminate against people based on race, color, ethnicity, sexual preference, creed, or religion, you know."

"Where do you think you fall on that list?" I said.

"Creed. I've sworn an oath to uphold the moral and ethical standards of the funeral arts community and to practice my craft with dignity and respect. That's called a 'creed' and maybe you're prejudiced against me for it."

"Trish, I can assure you one-hundred percent I'm not discriminating against you. I'm totally onboard to do your December wedding, but I simply can't meet with you today. If you could stay over for a day or two maybe we could meet tomorrow."

"I've already got departed loved ones stacking up in my embalming room back home. There's no way my boss will let me take more time off."

"Well, I understand your time constraints since you only have a little over a month, but—"

"You think I'm getting married *this* Christmas?"

"Yes, I thought you said—"

"No, silly. Buddy proposed for us to get married *next* year. I'm going to need at least a year to figure out everything I want and make sure it's absolutely perfect. Who in their right mind would have a wedding in only a month?"

I could've told her I could fill a book with stories of crazy brides wanting hurry-up weddings, but I chose to simply stick with the subject at hand. "Well then, we have plenty of time. How about I send you a really nice wedding planning album, where you can start writing down all your ideas and paste in pictures of the things you love? I'll also get you subscribed to *Hawaii Bride*. It's a beautiful magazine dedicated solely to brides doing destination weddings in the islands."

"Okay. I was hoping to meet with you before I go, but I guess that'll have to do."

"Don't worry, this is actually a good thing. In the wedding industry we see so many changes from year to year. What's trendy this Christmas will be passé by next. We should meet no earlier than six months out from your wedding date. That way, you can be assured of having only the freshest, most up-to-the-minute trends and styles."

"Hmm. I guess that makes sense," she said.

Once again, I'd BS'd my way out of a tight spot.

"Great," I said. "Send me an email when you get home with your street address and I'll be sure to get that wedding album and magazine subscription on their way to you right away."

"Okay. So, I guess I'll see you next summer."

"Looking forward to working with you, Trish."

"Me too. Oh, and Pali?"

"Yeah?"

"Please try real hard to stay out of jail. At least until after my wedding."

"Will do." I gave her a half-hearted chuckle and hung up.

I got out of the car and listened. I strained to hear screams—either ancient or modern—but the only sound was the brisk valley wind rustling leaves on the trees. I got back inside and checked my watch: I still had forty minutes to go.

I turned the radio on to my favorite station, KPOA-FM, and they were playing a goofy song about partying all weekend and dreading work on Monday. I thought about Beni singing the beer bottle song and it hit me: I should use my time waiting for Ono to figure out how long it had taken Beni to get to the campsite.

I pulled out my cell phone and punched through the menu until I got to the stop watch feature. I started singing. I sang the song slowly, like Farrah had demonstrated. It took me fifteen seconds to finish one stanza. If Beni went from ninety-nine to thirteen, that meant he sang eighty-six stanzas, more or less. I then found the calculator on the cell phone and punched in the numbers. Assuming Beni hadn't stopped singing while he was hiking, the calculator gave me an answer of twenty-one and a half minutes. He'd probably taken a few breaths between stanzas so that could've added a minute or two. So, a rough estimate was it should take us between twenty-one and twenty-five minutes to get to the campsite. Less than half an hour? I was glad I'd taken time to figure it out—it lifted my spirits a little. I mean, how hard could it be to find a place that was only a half-hour away?

I was daydreaming when Ono came up and rapped on the window. He'd looped a khaki canvas daypack over one shoulder and was wearing camo print cargo shorts and a black tee-shirt. I considered giving him some grief over his 'Rambo-style' get-up, but let it go. After all, it was early Sunday morning; if I hadn't called, he'd probably still be snug in his bunk.

I got out and he gave me a quick hug. "How ya doin'?" he said.

"As well as can be expected, I guess. What's the idea you were working on before you came up here?"

"It's not a done deal yet. I'll let you know if it pans out."

We trudged up the road to the park entrance and I looked around. It was not yet eight thirty, but a smattering of visitor cars were already parked in the lot.

The park was densely wooded, so it was hard to tell where the tourists were, but most visitors head directly for the steps leading up to the vantage point for the 'Iao Needle. The needle isn't really a spike-like rock formation—it's more an optical illusion. From the overlook it looks like a single spire of rock but it's really the thin end-piece of a massive rock ridge that runs along the valley. From the viewing platform you can see beautiful views of the stream as it winds its way up into the valley. Turn around and you're looking down slope into the mouth of the valley as it opens out to the flatlands beyond Wailuku.

Ono and I took the trail to the left. It was a rather steep paved walkway down to fast-rushing 'Iao Stream.

"Water looks pretty deep," he said.

"Yeah, well as my Auntie Mana used to say, 'You're not sugar—you won't melt'."

"I wasn't worried about melting," he said. "What worries me is if you lose your footing on one of these boulders, I'll probably have to go down and fish you out of Kahului Bay."

"Me? I'm the one with the black belt, remember? I can balance on the head of a pin."

"Great. But let's see how well you balance on a slippery round rock with a hundred gallons of water rushing around it. You want to take my hand?"

"No, I think we'll both have a better chance going it on our own."

"You first, or me?"

"Are you stalling, Kingston? 'Cuz it sounds to me like you're the one worried about getting wet."

With that, he hopped onto the first rock—balanced for a few seconds—and then hopped onto the next. I followed. At first I focused on the dirt embankment on the other side of the swiftly-moving stream, but I soon figured out it was easier to focus on the next rock—and then the one after that—in order to plan my next move.

About halfway across, I balanced on a steeply sloped boulder with an uneven top. I tried to maintain my footing as I watched the flashing stream roar around me. The din of the rushing water swept away all other sound. I felt suspended in an alternate universe of enveloping white noise, a swiftly shifting landscape of blue-black water, and bracing clear air.

I heard someone yell above the roar and I looked to the opposite side. Ono had already made it across. His face was pinched and frowning. He held out his hand as if reaching to pull me forward. I could just barely hear what he was shouting at me.

"You okay? You need me to come back and get you?"

I shook my head, and in doing so I lost my balance. I felt my foot sliding—almost as if in slow-motion—off the boulder and then into the stream. In a split second I was thigh-deep in the frigid water. I quickly grabbed onto the misshapen rock and pulled myself up, but my pants and sneakers were soaked.

"I'll come—" Ono started to say, but I cut him off.

"No! Stay there. I'm fine."

I hopped across the rest of the rocks and grabbed Ono's outstretched hand to hoist myself onto the bank.

"You okay?" Ono said. "How about your phone? Is it still working?"

I pulled my cell phone from my pocket. It wasn't damaged, but it showed no service in the area.

"My phone's fine. And I'm good. We're both a little damp, but as my Auntie Mana would say—"

"Yeah, so I've heard. Why don't you give me the phone and I'll put it in my backpack. That way it can't fall out of your pocket."

We slipped through the bushes and small trees that grew thick along the bank. It was slow going, since there was no trail, only dense foliage and basketball-size rocks we had to maneuver around. The terrain was steep and I couldn't imagine Beni singing—even silently—as he made his way through this dense thicket while trudging up the sharp incline.

I checked my watch: four minutes to ten. If we were on the right track we should come across the campsite at about twenty after ten. I wasn't in any hurry to see what waited for me there, but I was eager to get it over with.

Every now and then the thick brush and trees would open up to a small area with flat ground covered by thin clumps of grass. We'd move through the flat area quickly and be back to hacking through foliage in less than a minute. The brilliant green of the valley was almost hard on my eyes. I'd learned in school that 'Iao Valley is in a rain forest which gets nearly four hundred inches of rain per year at the top of the Pu'u Kukui summit. Most of the rain drains into the 'Iao Stream, but a lot of it soaks into the ground making it possible for the thousands of bushes and trees to grow tightly packed together.

We didn't talk much. Ono kept looking back to check if I was still in sight but then he'd move on. It almost seemed as if he had a schedule to keep, but maybe he felt like I did and just wanted to get this whole wretched ordeal over with.

My soggy cropped pants stuck to my legs and my sneakers squished with every step but the air temperature was warm. The exertion of the constant uphill climb stoked my body heat. I kept checking my watch. At ten after ten I slowed down and started checking out the landscape, looking for recently disturbed soil. Ono turned to look back, saw I'd fallen behind and stopped. He didn't look too pleased with my dallying, but I didn't care. If we overshot our destination we'd end up hopelessly lost.

At a quarter after ten, the terrain flattened out. We'd entered a small meadow about the size of the lot my house sits on in Hali'imaile. Trees framed the sides of the meadow, but in the center the ground was level, with soft red soil covered by a thin layer of grass.

Ono reached into his daypack and pulled out my cell phone. He used it to take a few pictures of the meadow, then turned and snapped one of me. He didn't need to tell me to smile because I already was. Thanks to Beni's silly drinking song we'd safely arrived at the perfect place to dig a grave.

# 26

Except there was no grave. Nor was there a single shred of evidence that a former campsite had been anywhere near there. We scoured the area like two people searching for a lost contact lens but we came up short on all counts.

"Did we make a wrong turn?" I said.

"How could we make a wrong turn?" said Ono. "There was only one way to go."

"Except we crossed the stream at the low point in the park and then headed up the valley from there."

"Yeah, so?" said Ono. He looked like he was waiting for me to smack my forehead and admit I'd just remembered Beni hadn't said 'Iao Valley, but rather *Waihe'e* Valley, which is miles away on the north shore.

"Well, the 'Iao Stream splits down by the park," I said. "Maybe Beni was talking about a different fork of the stream— like down by the footbridge. If he went up into the valley from there, he would've ended up in a totally different place."

Ono stared up at the sky for half a minute before answering. "Remember when I told you I needed a couple hours to check out an idea?"

"Yeah."

"Well, I've got a buddy who owes me a favor. I think it's time to call it due."

We made our way back down to the park in no time. It always seems that way; it takes forever to go someplace and then you can get back in a flash. We crossed the stream at the same place we had earlier and this time I didn't dally, and I didn't fall in.

"You want to go up that way—into the other side of the valley?" I said, pointing at the other branch of the stream as we crossed over the footbridge.

"Nah. Let's just go on down to my car. I need to make a call."

We walked down the road and he stopped next to an ancient VW van. It was two-tone, red on the bottom and dirty white on the top. It looked like it'd been up on blocks for at least a couple of decades—lots of rust damage and a sun-bleached paint job that made it look pink in spots.

"Wow, dude," I said. "I'm glad to see there's someone on this island with a sadder-looking ride than mine."

"Hey," he said, "these wheels are classic. Nineteen sixty-four VW bus, nearly one-hundred percent stock—inside and out. Even the color's stock: sealing wax red and beige grey. It's hard to come by one of these babies that's still running."

"Well, I gotta admit, I've got a girlfriend up in Pa'ia who'd go absolutely *pupule* over your little hippie bus. Where'd you get it?"

"Bought it off an old *auntie* up in Makawao. She said her husband hung on to it after their son got killed in the war."

"Iraq or Afghanistan?" I asked.

"Nah, way back in Vietnam. Seems the son bought it new and his father couldn't bear to part with it. But now the old guy's dead too . I rebuilt the engine. It runs great, but I'm not so good with body work. It's quite the conversation piece wherever I go. I had a guy come up to me at Costco a few weeks ago and offer to trick it up like a 'hippie love wagon'—you know, throw on some peace signs and doves and stuff. I told him the faded paint and rust holes were hippie enough for me."

"My folks were hippies," I said. "Real hard core. In the '70's they lived up in the trees at Taylor's Camp on Kauai. I wonder what they'd have thought of the stuff we have now—you know, cell phones and Internet dating."

"Your folks are no longer around?"

"No. I was 'little orphan Pali' at a pretty young age."

"That's too bad. But if they were anything like my folks I can give you a hint how they'd be now. Back in the day, my folks were hard-core hippies too. Free love, organic everything, a couple of 'special plants' under grow lights in the basement. Now they live on an Arizona golf course, take country-western dance lessons, and typically eat dinner around four o'clock in the afternoon."

He pulled out a huge wad of keys and unlocked the passenger door. I crawled up onto the cracked leatherette seat. The van even smelled hippie—like a gunny sack full of mangoes that'd been left outside on a hot day.

He got in on his side and pulled a cell phone from under the driver's seat. He flipped it open and hit a speed-dial number. "Gordon? Yeah, it's me again. I'm afraid I'm gonna have to ask you to fire it up." There was a pause and then he said, *"Mahalo.* We'll be down in a flash."

He snapped the phone shut and turned to me. "You think you can handle going out to the airport? I hear your name's been added to the no-fly list, so if you wanna skip it, just say the word." He laughed. I didn't.

The VW van seemed to have a maximum speed of about forty. Cars zipped around us as we headed down out of Wailuku into Kahului and then out onto the airport road. Ono was conscientious and chugged along in the right lane, even pulling onto the shoulder if people tried to pass when there was oncoming traffic.

"Are you going to fill me in on why we're going to the airport?" I said.

"We're gonna do some reconnaissance. 'Recon' that will probably save us time and sweat." He turned right at Old Haleakala Highway.

"I thought we were going to the airport," I said. "You turned too soon."

"No, we're going to the other side of the runway."

I didn't question him. I'd been to that side of the airport earlier in the year. It's where the private planes land.

"We're going to the private terminal?"

"Close. We're going to the heliport, where the choppers are based."

I perked up. I'd flown countless hours in commercial jets as a federal air marshal but I'd never been up in a helicopter. "Are we going for a ride?"

"Yep. I've got a friend who's offered us a flyover of 'Iao Valley. I want to see if we can spot anything from the air."

"I suppose under the circumstances it's kind of tacky to say 'yippee'."

"Regardless of the circumstances, I think 'yippee,' is in order," he said. "I can never decide which I love more: sailing Tomika's cat or flying in one of Gordon's birds."

"You ever wish you could own something like that yourself—you know, a catamaran or maybe a little private plane?"

"You know, I've thought about it, but it never pencils out. The maintenance, the insurance premiums, the fuel cost. At this point in my life I'm content being the sidekick—the friend with benefits."

We got to the heliport and parked. There were three helicopters waiting on the tarmac. A guy in a dark blue jumpsuit waved us over to the far left helicopter and when we got there, he and Ono gave each other a 'man hug'—one of those shoulder-to-shoulder things followed by a couple of slaps on the back.

"Hey, my man, you didn't mention you were bringing a co-pilot," said the jumpsuit guy.

"Pali Moon, this is my friend Gordon Walker. Pali's a local. She's acquainted with the girl we're looking for up at 'Iao."

I couldn't help but notice that Ono played down Crystal's dire circumstances for his friend.

"Good to meet you, Pali," said Gordon. "You been hanging around this salty dog for long?"

"No," I said. "We just met a couple of weeks ago. I booked the *Maui Happy Returns* for some mainland clients of mine."

"Then she helped me sail the cat over to O'ahu for Tomika," Ono said. "She's a solid co-captain. And, she's flown for the feds—mostly Homeland Security stuff."

I wasn't sure why Ono was glitzing up my resumé, but I went along.

"Good. You ever fly choppers?" Gordon said.

I waited for Ono to answer, then realized Gordon was talking to me.

"Uh, no. Not much chopper experience."

"Well, no worries. Ono here has probably forgot more'n I'll ever know. But you think you'll be okay in the second seat?"

Okay, I'm not stupid. I could see where this was going. I nodded. I figure lying's a little more acceptable if it's done silently.

"Great. Well, she's all gassed up and checked out. But you two will want to do your own pre-flight checks, I'm sure."

"*Mahalo, brudda*. I owe you a cold one," said Ono.

"Dude, you could fly this thing all the way to Japan and I'd still have a ways to go to pay you back for everything you've done for me," said Gordon. "But I'll take you up on that beer sometime. It'd be good to catch up."

Another man hug and Gordon loped off toward a little free-standing building with a neon orange wind sock flapping from a pole on the roof.

"You want to fill me in on what just happened?" I said.

"We're gonna take this bird up and look around for your girl." Ono's grin told me he was proud of his little performance—and mine.

"Well, then let's do it."

***

I strapped myself in and put on my ear muffs. Ono flipped switches on the dash and started talking to the tower at Kahului Airport. He got clearance to head out and the next thing I knew we were up and away.

Flying in a helicopter is nothing like flying in a commercial jet. It's not even like being in a small two-seater plane. Helicopters feel like they have more in common with elevators than anything with fixed wings. They go up—straight up. No fooling around with taxiing, no slow climb from the runway to reach flying altitude. The steady *whomp, whomp, whomp* of the rotor blades reminded me we were traveling in a machine and not something extraterrestrial, but the helicopter lifted so effortlessly it was almost as if it were immune to gravity.

"Whew! This is fantastic," I said. "I feel lighter than air."

"I know. I love it. In the Army I flew Uncle Sam's big Bell copters, but flying a little sightseeing chopper like this is like driving a fancy sports car. Keep a sharp eye out, we'll be over 'Iao Valley in no time."

He was right. We were moving much faster than we ever could've on land, and within a few minutes we'd left Kahului and Wailuku behind and were entering the lush green of the valley.

"What are we looking for?" I asked.

"Didn't you say Beni said your girl was in a blue tent? Maybe it's still there."

"Yeah. But I don't know what color blue. It could be dark blue, baby blue, turquoise blue, or..."

"Doesn't matter. If you see anything blue, sing out."

We swooped in low over the ridge of the 'Iao Needle and I grabbed the edge of my seat in alarm.

"Coming in a little low there, cowboy," I said.

"Nah, don't worry. We're not as close to the ground as it looks. And the altimeter bell will go off if I get too hold-ass crazy. We gotta stay low if we hope to see anything from up here."

We zipped along and it seemed to me that even if there was anything worth seeing it would flash by too quickly for us to notice.

Then I saw it.

# 27

I pointed to the four o'clock position in the front bubble window of the cockpit and Ono nodded. A bright smudge of royal blue contrasted against the mottled green of the carpet of foliage below.

"Do you think that's it?" I said, squinting my eyes to peer at the blue blotch.

"I'm gonna take her around again and see if I can get in a little lower."

"Lower?" My voice sounded squeaky through the mic system in the ear muffs.

"Not too much lower. Just enough to see if we can get a fix on a surrounding landmark."

There weren't many landmarks. The dense tropical forest stretched on and on—a bumpy topography of tree-tops and dark green hillside brush for as far as the eye could see.

We hovered above the small patch of blue for a few seconds. Ono blew out a breath and then dipped the chopper down a bit lower.

"Hang on," he said. "We're good, but I'm trying to get a bead on pinpointing the stream from here. If I can locate the stream in relation to this blue thing, we'll have a shot at finding our way back here on foot."

The stream turned out to be only a short distance to the west of the blue spot.

"Just like you thought," he said. "We're over the opposite fork of the 'Iao Stream. This isn't the side we were on this morning."

He tapped one of the cockpit dials, then maneuvered the stick to take us up a little higher. As we hovered over the spot, he scribbled a note on a tiny notepad clipped to the instrument panel.

"We're good. Let's take 'er back now," he said.

I shot him my best sad-faced *do we have to?* look.

"Okay. I'll take you on a quick spin over the West Side before we buzz on in. I promised Gordy we'd be gone less than an hour. He doesn't mind sharing his chopper, but paying for the fuel's another thing."

We flew all the way through the 'Iao Valley, then dipped and followed the Launiupoko Valley until we popped out on the leeward side of the island. I could see Lahaina Town to my right and a huge tract of glittering ocean straight ahead. The islands of Lana'i and Molokai lay ahead on the horizon, their tops still shrouded in clouds. Just at the point where the earth curved away from view I spotted what I think was the uppermost point of Diamond Head on O'ahu. Ono steered left and from that vantage I was able to make out the stark brown landscape of the uninhabited island of Kaho'olawe, just off the southern tip of Maui. I knew the Big Island of Hawaii lay somewhere further south, but it wasn't visible. Below me lay a dazzling expanse of diamond-studded ocean quivering beneath a fierce blue sky.

I didn't say a word. There was nothing to say that would capture the awe I felt at that moment.

\*\*\*

By the time we landed it was almost one o'clock, which gave us plenty of time to go back into the valley to check if the blue smudge we'd seen from the air was the tent in the campsite we'd been looking for. But I was hungry.

"*Mahalo* for the ride," I said as Ono helped me out of the cockpit. "I think we've got something to shoot for, but before we go back up there, can I buy you lunch?"

"Gordy loaning me his chopper, you buying me lunch— this day just keeps getting better and better," Ono said with a smile. "Where do you want to go?"

"You like *saimin?*"

"Sure. Who doesn't?"

"You ever been to Sam Sato's up in Wailuku? It's right on our way back up to 'Iao Valley. It's nothin' fancy but he's got *broke da mouth* good *saimin.*"

"Sounds like a plan."

We made it to the *saimin* place in twenty minutes and were served and back out on the road in another thirty. Ono's van chugged back up to the entrance to 'Iao Valley State Park but this time we had to park much further down the road since the place was now teeming with tourists.

"Do you think we should try this with so many people around?" I said.

"Nobody's gonna be looking at us. Let's play like we're lovers looking for a little afternoon delight. I hear this is a popular spot for that kinda thing." He grinned.

"Sounds like the voice of experience," I said.

"I told you, I come from hippie stock. We're big into getting back to nature."

We held hands and lolled around the footbridge waiting for it to clear off before ducking below. As we scrambled through the thick brush it occurred to me we'd probably never find the blue tent—the landscape was so overgrown it was impossible to see more than a few feet ahead.

"Ono, this is ridiculous. We could be out here for hours and still miss that tent by half a mile."

"Not hardly," he said. He swung his pack off his shoulder and pulled out the little note he'd jotted down in the helicopter. Then from a different pocket he dug out a device about the size of a cell phone. He fired it up and showed me the display.

"Global positioning," he said, punching in numbers. "This baby's accurate to within ten feet. From the looks of things, we're right on track."

We slogged on. This time we didn't cross the stream, but instead kept to the right of it as we hiked up the steep terrain. We passed a couple of small clearings, and as we approached each one, Ono checked his GPS device and then shook his head.

At last we arrived within the hot zone of the GPS coordinates.

"Keep an eye out. It's gotta be right around here somewhere," he said.

We pushed through the brush and came out at a narrow rock-strewn trail.

"This looks promising," I said. "Why didn't we see this trail before?"

"Don't know," said Ono. "It looks like it's been pretty well traveled. In fact, check this out: looks like we may not be the first people up here today."

He pointed to a muddy shoe print traveling in the direction we were headed.

"How do you know that print's not a week old?" I said. "It could be from the kidnappers—or Beni."

"This is a rain forest," he said. "It rains nearly every day—especially this time of year. This print is fresh—no more than a day old."

"So while we were chowing down at Sam Sato's someone else might have beaten us to the campsite?"

He put his finger to his lips to noiselessly tell me to *shush*.

We stepped back into the trees and crouched down. I peered through the thick brush. I couldn't see much, but within a few seconds I heard men's voices coming our way.

"...not likely, *brudda*," said one guy. His voice sounded local.

"What you think?" said another guy.

"...up here not so easy to find..." The wind rustling the leaves made it difficult to catch the whole conversation.

Ono and I stayed silent and hidden. My thighs were starting to burn by the time the guys came within earshot.

"I tol' you this was a waste of time. The wife gave me a ton of *kaumaha* about ducking out on a Sunday." It was the first guy's voice.

"You think they'll close the park?" said the second guy.

The other guy laughed. "No worries to me. I still get paid."

"Man, maybe we should look around a little more. I don't want no trouble with the cops."

"No, I gotta get home. It's my *keiki* nephew's birthday. Nothing's gonna..." and then their voices drifted away.

We stayed hidden for another half-minute to make sure they didn't circle back, then we stood and stretched.

"Whew. That felt like a million thigh squats," I said. "My Sifu Doug makes us do those if we whine during practice."

"Well, now we have some idea who made the shoe print we saw earlier," said Ono. "And it sounds like they were up there looking for something. We need to get a move on."

Later, I couldn't help thinking about how my life would've been different if we hadn't found the kidnappers' campsite. I'm a pretty good wedding planner for a lot of reasons, but mostly it's because I'm detail-oriented and have great visual memory. I see something once and it sticks. As we made our way up the trail to the campsite, I tried to imagine what we'd find once we got there. I pictured a tidy little mound of freshly-turned earth, with maybe a little circle of stones marking a final resting place. I steeled myself to deal with finding a sandal, maybe a piece of ripped clothing, or some other distressing clue to Crystal's final struggle. What I was totally unprepared for was seeing just how vicious people could be. With each step I came closer to creating an enduring memory that still haunts me each time I close my eyes to sleep.

As they say, you can't un-ring a bell.

# 28

The campsite was a mess—broken bottles strewn around; a barely-covered latrine hole that stunk to high heaven; and the collapsed blue tent flapping in the wind like a huge bird foundered by a broken wing. We took it all in but stayed back.

"This is a crime scene," I said. "I think we need to locate the grave, take a few pictures, and then get the hell out of here."

"Yeah," said Ono. "Except for the 'head hole' the dirt in this area looks pretty intact. No grave here."

"Beni said he was ordered to dig some distance away. He said when he finished he went *down* to where they were holding Crystal."

"Okay," said Ono, "why don't you circle around that way to the left and I'll circle right and let's see what we come up with."

Left was uphill from the campsite so I wasn't surprised when I was the one who first spotted the freshly-turned earth. The hole was shallow—maybe two or three feet deep. It was still open; no one had bothered to fill it back up with the mound of dirt piled nearby. Maybe Beni had been right in assuming the drug dealers had chased him as he'd fled the scene. Or, maybe they were just such inhumane dirt-bags that they'd purposely left Crystal's body exposed to the elements so it would decay faster. It didn't matter. There it was, a body-sized bundle, wrapped in a dirty sheet.

"Ono," I yelled. "She's up here."

He thrashed through the brush and joined me. We both gazed down at the bundle.

"You think that's her?" he said.

"Who else?" I'd seen enough. Although the body looked small, lying in the open grave, there was no doubt in my mind we'd finally found Crystal Wilson.

"We better take a look," said Ono. He knelt down and grasped an edge of the sheet. I looked away.

"This her?"

I reluctantly turned back.

He'd pulled the sheet away from her head. She was face-up, her skin the color of day-old *poi*. Above her closed eyes, dead center in her forehead, were two dime-sized black holes. I sucked in a breath. The last thing she'd seen on this Earth must've been the callous face of her executioner. I could only hope she'd closed her eyes as a final gesture of defiance—to rob her killer of the satisfaction of watching the panic in her eyes as he pulled the trigger.

I turned away again. I'd seen enough. Later, Ono would recall the full extent of Crystal's injuries and the state of her body after almost a week in the hole, but I spared myself the details.

"What do you want to do now?" said Ono as we stood alongside the gravesite. I appreciated him saying that. He was used to issuing orders; being a boat captain and all. But this was my predicament and he respected that.

"Let's take a few photos and get out of here. I'd like to report this before those guys on the trail say anything. Who do you suppose they were?"

"My best guess is they're park workers," Ono said. "You heard the one guy say he'd get paid even if they closed the park? Sounded like a dedicated public servant—Maui-style."

"Would you mind taking the pictures?" I said. "I'm kind of having a hard time here."

"No problem." He rummaged around in his backpack and pulled out my cell phone. Then he leaned over the open hole and snapped half a dozen shots.

"Any other photos you think we should get while we're here?" he said.

I pointed to the debris-strewn campsite below. "Probably ought to take a few establishing shots. I want to make sure Detective Wong has everything he needs to work on this, and nothing he can use to make excuses."

"It's still hard to believe Wong shut you down again and again. Seems to me you brought him some pretty solid leads— the hair and fingernails—not to mention that ransom note."

"Yeah, well if I've learned anything in my prior dealings with the man, it's that it's Wong's way or the highway. I'll bet his partner's got a few stories about what a pleasure he is to work with."

Ono took a few more pictures while I checked the perimeter of the campsite for additional evidence. Aside from the garbage tossed around and the crumpled tent there wasn't much there. I didn't really expect they'd leave drugs or a gun behind, but if I could've spotted some shell casings or other proof of what had happened, and where, it would've helped corroborate Beni's story.

We took the trail on the way back down. It was much easier than crashing through the underbrush but once we got to the bottom I realized why we hadn't noticed it before. It didn't end at the park, but rather looped around and brought us to a gate in a six-foot tall chain-link fence. There was a small green plantation-style house about ten yards away.

"This is strange," I said.

"Yeah," said Ono. He tried the latch on the gate. It rattled but didn't give way.

The sound must've alerted the on-site security, because within seconds a powerfully-built American Staffordshire Terrier—aka a pit bull—was snarling at us only inches away on his side of the chain link. Although he was slobbering and baring his teeth, he looked almost happy; as if he was thrilled to finally have the opportunity to strut his stuff.

"We better go back," I said.

Ono made no move to leave. Instead, he bent down and started making a strange noise deep in his throat. It sounded as if he was trying to communicate with the dog in some kind of visceral dog language.

"Are you nuts?" I said. "Dogs like this don't live alone, you know." I looked at the house, half expecting a wild-eyed guy brandishing a machete to burst through the back door.

Ono kept up the goofy throat noise. I stepped back a few feet and watched.

After half a minute, the dog stopped growling. It perked up its ears as if trying to decode the message Ono was sending. Then it sat down on its haunches, its eyes focused on Ono as if waiting for him to throw a ball.

"What're you doing?" I said.

"I'm dog whispering. I learned it from a guy who trains sled dogs up in Alaska."

"We don't have time for you to sweet-talk this dog. Especially since he's probably only playing along while he figures out whether to go with the béarnaise or the hollandaise sauce on your upper arm."

"Okay." He stood and turned away from the dog. Just like that, the dog leapt up and crashed against the fence. He resumed his rip-your-face-off snarling and barking with even greater vigor.

"I think I hurt his feelings by acting as if I wanted to be friends and then not following through," said Ono.

"Well, it'll hurt *my* feelings if we stick around here long enough for that ninety-eight pounds of pissed-off to find a hole in this fence."

We hacked our way back through the brush and found our cars.

"Should we call the cops and have them meet us up here?" said Ono.

"Nope. I want to march into that station unannounced. I don't want to give up the element of surprise when I show Wong these pictures. No way he'll be able to stonewall me now."

\*\*\*

Since it was Sunday the police station lot was nearly empty except for a couple of cop cars parked out front. I waited for Ono to pull in behind me and park, then we walked together up to the door. I had to press a buzzer to be let inside. Once we got in, I asked the cop at the front desk to please page Detective Wong.

"Investigative services only works normal business hours," said the guy. "They're off today."

"I need to speak to Detective Wong regarding a missing persons report I filed on the first of the month," I said. "Please tell him I now have solid proof of foul play."

"And your name is?"

I told him my name. It always makes me nervous to give my chosen name to the police or any other people in authority. I'm waiting for the day when someone leaps up, thrusts an accusing finger in my face and calls me a big fat liar. It hasn't happened yet, but you never know.

The desk cop pointed to a row of plastic chairs lining the wall. "Please have a seat, Ms. Moon. I'll do my best to get a hold of him."

"I've never been in here before," said Ono. "God knows I've seen my share of police stations, but I somehow managed to avoid this one."

The cop mumbled something into his headset and then looked up at me. "Detective Wong said to tell you he's on his way. If you want something to drink there's a vending machine down the hall. Or, if you need to use the restroom I can give you the key."

"*Mahalo*, but we're fine. Any idea how long it'll take Detective Wong to get here?"

"He said he was close by," said the clerk. His console started beeping and he looked down, probably relieved to be able to direct his attention elsewhere. My money says Wong isn't anybody's 'Mr. Congeniality' and most likely he'd yelled at the guy for calling him in.

Glen Wong didn't come through the front doors, but suddenly appeared behind the counter where the desk clerk sat.

"Ms. Moon, I see you're not alone. Is this your lawyer?"

I looked over at Ono in his cargo shorts and black tee-shirt and wondered how Wong could possibly mistake the guy for an attorney.

"You're gonna probably need one, that's all," said Wong.

"Why?"

"Because I see an obstruction of justice charge in your future."

"What?"

"We had a deal, right? You promised to leave this missing person investigation up to us. The mere fact that you're here—on a Sunday, no less—makes me assume you've broken that agreement."

"I'm here with undeniable proof that a crime's been committed," I said. "I'm a private citizen doing her civic duty, nothing more. To imply that I'm guilty of obstruction of anything is just plain—"

"Ms. Moon, not following a police order is against the law. And it's a crime to harbor a known fugitive who's wanted for police questioning. Do you need me to go on?"

I bit my lip and looked over at Ono. He shrugged.

"I'll get us an interview room," said Wong. "Follow me."

Ono stood up, but Wong held up his hand like a cop stopping traffic. "If you know what's good for you, you'll stay out of this. I'm gonna let you walk out of here this time—no harm, no foul—but I'd suggest you forget all about whatever harebrained story you've been told by Ms. Moon. If it gets back to me you've not taken this advice, Ms. Moon won't be the only one needing a lawyer."

Ono looked at me. His eyes were troubled—as if he was worried I'd think less of him if he didn't posture and bluff in a manly show of protecting me from this bully.

"Go," I said. "I shouldn't have dragged you into this in the first place."

Ono slipped off his backpack, pulled out my cell phone and handed it to me. "Here," he said. "Good luck."

Wong muttered something I couldn't quite hear.

Ono glared at Wong. "You're a pathetic excuse for a cop, you know that? This woman is doing the job you should've been doing two weeks ago. Now you're gonna see what happened as a result of your arrogance. And believe me, if you so much as harm a—"

"Let's not go there, buddy," said Wong. "Ms. Moon and I are going to sit down for a little chat, that's all. She'll be outta here in no time." He turned to me. "Do you have your own ride home?"

I nodded.

"Good. Then I suggest you tell your friend to leave. You can give him a call when we're through."

I nodded again and Ono stomped toward the front door.

Wong led me down the hall and opened the door to the first interview room. He gestured for me to go in ahead of him. I took a seat and he sat on the opposite side of the table.

"Okay, why are you here?" he said.

"I want to show you some pictures that back up everything I've been saying for the past two weeks."

"Do you want to make a formal statement?"

"I guess so."

"Okay, then begin. I'll be recording what you say. We'll have it transcribed and you can sign it later."

In my statement I left out everything pertaining to Beni, saying instead that I'd heard a rumor in town about Crystal being held up in 'Iao Valley. I told Wong that Ono and I had gone up there and found the campsite and the open grave. When I got to the part about seeing her body, I choked up a little but managed to pull out my phone and flick through the photos Ono had taken and held each one up for Wong to see. When we got to the close-up of the two shots in Crystal's skull, he leaned in but didn't change his expression.

"Is that it?" said Wong.

"*Is that it*—are you joking? I'm showing you pictures of a murdered woman and you're asking me if that's *it*?"

"No, I mean, is this your entire statement?"

"Yeah. I think that's plenty, don't you?"

Wong picked my phone up off the table. He punched the buttons, scrolling once more through each of the photos. Now and then he stopped to scrutinize a shot before moving on. I waited, not saying anything.

"Pretty impressive police work, wouldn't you say, Detective?" I said. I didn't care that it sounded snotty. I was waiting for him to thank me—or at least offer some shred of appreciation for the irrefutable evidence I'd brought him. Now he had what he needed to launch a full investigation into the kidnapping and murder of Crystal Wilson.

"Mind if I make copies of these photos?" he said. "I'd like to download them to our system."

"Sure, whatever it takes."

He got up and left the room, then came back a few minutes later.

"By the way, did you enjoy your little helicopter ride, Ms. Moon?" he said, handing me my phone.

"How did you—"

"Ms. Moon, it seems you fail to remember even the most rudimentary information I pass along to you. Not long ago I told you it's my business to know who's on this island and what they're up to. Well, that includes locals—like you."

"You have no right—" I stammered.

"You're free to go now," he interrupted. "I suggest you call your friend, Mr. Winston, at your earliest convenience. When he left here he seemed rather concerned about your welfare."

When I got outside I was surprised to find Ono still in the parking lot, sitting in his bus. I walked over and he rolled down the window.

"That was quick," he said.

"Yeah, I gave him a statement, but mostly I let the pictures do the talking. He even downloaded them onto his computer. Looks like there's no way he can weasel out of this now."

"Pali?" he said.

Our eyes met. I could tell we were both thinking the same thing. I yanked my cell phone out of my pocket and punched buttons until I got to the pictures screen.

# 29

Of course the pictures weren't there. The most recent photos on my phone were shots I'd taken of Steve in his Halloween costume. He was going to a classic movie party and he'd dressed up as *Citizen Kane*. He'd bulked up his middle by wrapping a towel under a 1940's-style shirt and he'd found a great-looking fedora and a little fake mustache. I thought he looked great, but people at the party mistook him for the ruthless banker in *It's a Wonderful Life*.

"We need to go back to the valley," I said to Ono. "Before they—"

"Hop in."

By the time we reached the park they'd pulled the gate shut across the parking lot entrance. We parked along the road and hiked up to the park. A park ranger was stationed at the trail leading in.

"Sorry, the park's closed for the rest of the day," he said as we approached.

"Why?" said Ono.

"We got a problem up at the 'Iao Needle. Seems some big dude leaned too hard on the guard rail and it gave way. Gotta get it re-welded."

"How long will that take?" I asked.

"Who knows? You know how it goes. Could take an hour, could take a week," he smiled and shot us a *shaka* sign.

"We're not going anywhere near the needle," Ono said. "We left something on one of the upper trails. It's kind of valuable and we need to get it."

"Sorry, *brudda*, no can do. This whole place *kapu* until we get a green light from the big boss."

I couldn't be sure, but his voice sounded a lot like one of the two guys we'd heard when we were hiding in the bushes up on the trail.

The walkie-talkie on his belt squawked, and he put it up to his ear. He said some stuff like, *ten-four* and *roger that* and then he turned back to us. "I'm real sorry guys, but you gotta go now. We're getting ready to do a sweep of the park, to make sure everybody's out."

On the walk back to Ono's bus my cell phone chimed. I checked the caller ID—it was Bessie Yokamura. As much as I wanted to hear her whine and wheedle her way back into my good graces, I let it go to voicemail.

"Now what should we do?" I said to Ono.

"It's your party, you tell me."

"I need some time to think. Would you mind taking me back to my car at the police station?"

"No worries. I've done some of my best thinking in this bus. Maybe it'll work for you too."

By the time we got to the police station neither of us had come up with any brilliant ideas for recovering the evidence of Crystal's murder. Seeing the cop cars parked out front brought up ugly feelings of betrayal.

"How can that man live with himself?" I said.

"I gotta say, I've run into some questionable cops in my day, but this guy wins—hands down."

"It's mind-boggling to think Wong's in on this," I said, looking at the front door of the police station. "I mean, we're talking *murder.*"

"Yeah, but we're also talking drugs. There's a boatload of money in drugs. On both sides. The government spends *billions* of tax dollars fighting the so-called war on drugs. And meanwhile, the drug traffickers are raking in a hundred times that selling their crap to willing buyers."

I leaned over and gave Ono a kiss on the cheek before opening my door. "*Mahalo*, for everything. I'll call you."

He frowned. "What? We spend the whole day chasing bad guys and now you're just gonna kick me to the curb? How about we grab some dinner tonight—maybe take your mind off what we saw today."

"My mind will never be far from what we saw until Crystal Wilson gets justice. I'm sorry, but I'm not exactly in the mood to go out."

"But you've still gotta eat. How about I bring some take-out over to your place?"

"You know, that'd be great."

I gave him directions to my house and then hopped down and went to my car. I drove up up to Pa'ia and parked in front of Farrah's store. I hadn't heard from her, so Beni probably still hadn't surfaced, but I wanted to clue her in on what we'd found up in the valley and what Wong had done when we reported it.

\*\*\*

"What?" Farrah shrieked. "I can't believe this. You found that poor girl's body and the cops are in on getting her killed?"

"Looks like it," I said. "We've got to find Beni. He's a witness so he's our only hope. Tomorrow I'll contact Honolulu—the attorney general's office or state police or somebody over there—and see what they say. But I'll need Beni to confirm my story."

"I've put the word out all day here at the store. So far, nothing."

"Oh, guess who called me?"

"Hatch?" she said.

"Hardly. I think my Hatch days are over. I can't even imagine what he'll say when he hears how I spent my Sunday."

"You mean about you and Ono?"

"Take your pick—me and Ono, me finding Beni a safe haven, or me tromping through the woods looking for a dead girl murdered by drug scum. Any one of those things could be a deal breaker. Taken all together—well, it was nice knowing him."

"So, who called you?" Farrah said.

Just then my phone rang.

"Well, speak of the devil," I said looking at the caller ID. "It's Bessie Yokamura. Mind if I take this?"

Farrah grinned. "Go ahead. You deserve a laugh after what you've been through."

"Hey Pali," Bessie said in a cheery voice. "How's it going, girlfriend?"

"Not that great, Bessie. I'm still doing that hour-long commute to Lahaina every day. You know, what with gas prices and all, it's getting tough."

"Well then, I'm gonna make your day, *sista*. I've decided to reconsider the lease on your old shop space in our Pa'ia building. I got to thinking—weddings are very important to our native culture. Hawaiians have always respected lineage through marriage as an integral part of the warp and woof in the weave of our social fabric."

"I don't know, Bessie. As much as I hate that commute, I know how much you want your tourist office. By the way, how's that coming along?"

"Oh, it's going good—great, actually. Lots of interest. In fact, looks I'm going to need an even larger place in town. I'm calling you because I want to give you first dibs on your old space—before I put the word out to the many other interested parties who've contacted me."

"Hmm, I don't know. Even though it's a long drive, I'm getting really good rent down in Lahaina. It's a sublet, you know."

"How much are you paying?"

"Well, to tell you the truth, hardly anything. But that's not the big issue, of course."

"What's more important than the rent price?"

"Oh, I don't know. Maybe working above a fish restaurant is preferable to working above sacred ancestor bones."

After a beat the line went dead.

"She hung up on me," I said to Farrah.

"Huh, imagine that. You serious about staying down in Lahaina?"

"No way. But she's gotta know everyone in town's heard about that *heiau* being under here." We both looked down as if we could look right through the floorboards and see the pile of stones and bones. "It's gonna be impossible to rent that space to anyone from Pa'ia."

"Or pretty much anyone on the island," Farrah said. She picked a copy of the Sunday Edition of *The Maui News* from the stack on the counter. The headline read, 'Ancient Human Bones Uncovered in Pa'ia.'

"Wow, I wonder who tipped them off," I said.

"Yeah," said Farrah. "I wonder."

"Can I see it?"

"The *heiau*? Sure."

She pulled a key from a nail under the counter and grabbed a flashlight hanging by the back door. "Follow me. I'm getting to be a pretty good tour guide."

She unlocked the door to my old shop and as I went in my heart squeezed in my chest. I loved the place. It didn't smell like it had when I'd worked there. The fire and the water from the fire fight had pretty much ruined all the floors and walls. Everything had been stripped down and replaced with new. But the windows were where they should be, and the mahogany door out to Baldwin Street was still there. How many times had I sat at my desk, staring out those windows trying to come up with the perfect attendant's gifts or puzzling over a complicated seating chart for a rehearsal dinner?

Farrah stood quietly by while I wallowed in my reverie. I looked over at her and she lifted an eyebrow.

"Yeah, I'm okay," I said. "Where are the *iwi*?"

She crossed the room and dragged aside a three by five foot piece of plywood that covered a large hole in the floor.

"Down here." She flicked on the flashlight and shined it down into the crawlspace.

It took my eyes a minute to focus. Then I saw it: a pile of lava stones—maybe twenty or thirty—with a half-dozen bleached bones at the base.

"There you have it," she said. "I told Bessie to get a *kahuna* to come over and check it out but she refused. Said it would just make things worse—you know, people talking and all."

"Lucky for you," I said.

She shot me a quizzical look.

"Farrah."

"Yeah, Pali?"

"Anything you want to tell me?"

"I miss you being here."

"Yeah, and I miss you. So, what kind of bones are those?"

"*Pua'a*—pig. From that luau down on Ka'anapali Beach. I asked your sifu's brother who works there to save me some and he did."

"You were able to fool the historical society with a stack of volcano rocks and some pig bones?"

"Pretty pathetic, huh?" she said.

"No, pretty damn smart." I gave her a hug. "I probably should go."

"It kind of creeps me out that Beni just vanished," she said as she moved the plywood back into position. "You don't think he's gonna end up like Crystal, do you? I mean, he's a weird little dude, but he's Doug Kanekoa's cousin."

"When I get home I'll call Sifu Doug and tell him to get in touch with James. No way James should be talking to the cops after what happened today. Hopefully I'll be able to convince someone in Honolulu to come over here. Until then, James needs to think of a way to protect his client."

"Assuming his client ever shows up again."

I went out the front door and Farrah locked up behind me. I noticed a plain white Ford Fairlane parked across the street. There were two guys inside. I trotted over to see if either of them was Wong, but as soon as I approached, they took off.

I got in my car and headed for home. Even though I was still smiling from seeing Farrah's artful *heiau* hoax, inside I felt like I'd swallowed a sack of cement. I was knock-down tired. I'd been only five when my Auntie Mana told me my mother had died. At first I didn't believe her. For a week I did all kinds of superstitious things: I told myself if I ate all my dinner in less than ten minutes then mama would come back; or if I was nice to my little brother and gave him a long piggy-back ride in the back yard, mama would come to the window and smile at me.

It didn't work back then, and nothing I did now would erase the overwhelming sense of loss I felt at seeing Crystal's body. A beautiful young woman had been brutally executed by thugs who were still at large. My hometown police were hell bent on covering it up. And the only witness to the crime was in the wind—or worse. I choked up and my eyes started leaking as I drove home.

Damn, I hated feeling so helpless.

# 30

When I turned the corner to my block, a white Ford Fairlane was parked in front of my house. I pulled around back and came in through the kitchen door. There were voices coming from the living room, so I went to check.

"Here she is," said Steve. He beamed as if I'd popped out of a birthday cake.

"Are you stalking me?" I said, glaring at Detective Wong. He and his partner were seated on the sofa side-by-side; Steve was in an armchair across from them.

"Now, is that any way to greet our guests?" Steve said.

"They're not guests, Steve. They're just trying to cover their tracks."

Steve lurched out of his chair. "Would you two please excuse us?" He grabbed my arm and dragged me back through the swinging door into the kitchen.

"Are you insane?"

"No, I'm not. I haven't had a chance to tell you what your boy toy's been up to. Those two are running interference for whoever killed Crystal Wilson. I'm not sure why, but I think it has something to do with them being on the take from the local drug pushers."

"Uh-uh. No way. I don't believe it for a minute," he said. "Besides, that's a pretty serious allegation. You can't just go around spouting off stuff like that."

"Trust me, it's all backed up by facts."

Wong pushed the kitchen door open, startling us. "We don't have time to sit around while you two *talk story* back here. I need to have a word with Ms. Moon and then we'll be leaving."

Steve mumbled his good-byes and left out the back door. I returned to the living room and took the seat Steve had left. Wong resumed his seat next to his partner.

"Ms. Moon, I've been more than forthright with you about my expectations regarding this investigation and you've ignored me every step of the way. Now, I'm afraid, I'm going to have to impose sanctions."

I shot him my best bored teenager scowl.

"You called me to come into the station this afternoon on my day off. I came in, happy to take your statement. But now you've done your civic duty, or whatever you think it is, so it's time for you to back off—completely. I'm warning you: if you attempt to meddle in this matter any further, you'll force me to play hardball."

He probably expected me to ask him what he meant by that, but I just stared him down.

"I'm not messing around here, Ms. Moon. If I hear, see, or even suspect, that you've been snooping around or talking to anyone about this I will charge you with obstruction of justice and impeding an official police investigation."

"Yeah," I said. "You mentioned that before. I'm really scared."

"You should be. I can hold you for forty-eight hours."

"Ooh, that sounds cozy."

"This isn't a joking matter, Ms. Moon. I'm dead serious. No more bullshit, no more games." He stood and his partner followed suit. "Oh, and one more thing: I have reason to believe you've been harboring a wanted fugitive. That's also a crime punishable by jail time. Do yourself a favor and stick to your wedding cakes and bridal veils and leave the investigating to us. You hear me?"

I didn't answer, nor did I bother to get up and show them out.

I called Sifu Doug, but had to leave a message. "Sifu—this is Pali. I need you to call James and tell him *not* to talk to the cops about Beni for any reason. I repeat, call James as soon as you get this message and tell him the deal with the cops is off. I'll explain it all when you call me back."

Ten minutes later the phone rang. I picked up, expecting it to be Doug, but it wasn't. It was Hatch.

"Hey, how're you doing? I've been thinking of you," he said, his voice husky.

"I'm okay."

"I'm off today. Back on tomorrow. I was wondering if you'd like to go out and grab a bite, or maybe come over here for some wine and *pupus*. I miss you. And Heen's been missing you too."

"*Mahalo* for the offer, but tonight's not good. I'm not feeling a hundred percent. I think I'm going to turn in early."

"You sick?"

"Not big sick, just kinda hinky."

"You still worrying about that missing girl? I'm sure she's fine. Probably just went back to the mainland without telling anybody. I haven't seen anything on the news, have you?"

"No."

"So there you go. By the way, what'd you do this weekend? I was hoping you'd call. When you left the other night I was a mess. I'm sorry I flipped out on you like that."

"That's okay. I'm sorry you had to relive that."

"Maybe you're feelin' funky 'cuz we need to get together and do some making up."

"Sounds fun, but I'm just too tired. I really need to hit the hay—catch up on some sleep." The lying was beginning to take a toll and I was actually starting to feel kind of sick. "How about a raincheck?"

"Yeah, sure. I was hoping we could get together before I have to go back on shift, but that's okay. How 'bout you come by the station tomorrow if you're feeling better?"

"Sounds good."

I hung up feeling like a traitor. I'd spent the whole day with Ono and it never crossed my mind that Sunday was Hatch's day off. And lying about being sick was pretty low, but there was no way I could tell him the truth of what I'd been doing all day. I'd go by the fire station on Monday and try to make amends.

*** 

Ono pulled in front of the house a half-hour later carrying a big brown bag emblazoned with the Home Depot logo. Ever since Maui made plastic bags *kapu* on the island, most people carried around their own shopping bags or they recycled good paper ones. In any event, even though the bag said otherwise, I was pretty sure Ono hadn't picked up dinner at a big box hardware store.

"Hey, you found my house," I said as I opened the door.

"I hope you're in the mood for fish and chips."

"Always. Thanks for picking it up. It smells *ono*."

"How 'bout that—two *onos* for the price of one," he said. We went in the kitchen and he put the bag down on the table. "So hey, how're you doing? You still bummed out about what we saw today?" He leaned in and kissed me lightly on the lips.

"Yeah, that and more." I told him about Wong coming by the house. "He said he could throw me in jail for forty-eight hours."

"That dude worries me. Nothing worse than a crooked cop. But don't worry—you're this close to sewing it up." He pinched his thumb and forefinger together. "Once you get the state cops involved we'll see who's going to jail."

We sat down and Ono pulled out enough food to feed a pee-wee football team: two kinds of fish—*mahi-mahi* and *opak-apaka*, a small Styrofoam bucket of freshly chopped cole slaw, a white bag with about a pound of crisp fries, a coffee cup full of tartar sauce and two cold beers.

"I'm a little short on drinks," Ono said. "But there was a big line so I didn't want to ask her to go back for more."

"It's perfect," I said. "And besides, I've got beer here and a bottle of pretty decent wine."

We dug in and for the first time in days I didn't think about Crystal or Beni or drug dealers or crooked cops.

"I'm glad you're able to eat," said Ono. "Some people who see stuff like you saw today lose their appetite."

"What? Is that a nice way of saying I'm pigging out?" I wiped my chin.

He laughed. "No, I'm serious. I admire a woman who can roll with the punches."

"Oh, I roll. Believe me, these last few days I've been rolling like a Michelin on fresh blacktop."

I got up to clean up the mess and Ono came up behind me and put his arms around my waist. He leaned in to nuzzle my neck and I jumped.

"You sure you're okay? You seem kinda fidgety."

I turned around and looked into his soft blue eyes. His face started to lose shape, like I was seeing his reflection in a funhouse mirror.

"Hey, hey," he said, swiping a tear from my cheek. "What's this?"

"Nothing. I guess I'm not rolling as well as I'd like to think. I can't shake the image of Crystal's body lying in that hole. Oh, and thanks again for not making me take the pictures. I've never seen a dead body like that."

"Wish I could say the same. When I was on the streets, I saw more than my share of bodies. But first time or tenth, it never gets easy."

"I can't imagine you homeless. You seem so normal."

"There are a lot of *normal* people on the streets—war vets, guys out of work, even families who went broke taking care of a sick kid. Believe me, you don't choose that life, it chooses you."

He leaned in and kissed me. I wrapped my arms around his neck and kissed him back. After the heartache of the past few hours it felt better than I expected.

I wasn't quite ready to pull away when there was a knock at the front door.

"Probably one of Steve's friends," I said. "I'll just tell 'em he's down at the Ball & Chain. Don't move, I'll be right back."

As soon as I went through the kitchen door I recognized the face peeking through cupped hands at the picture window. He'd seen me too—no retreat.

"Hatch," I said, opening the door. "What're you—"

"I figured what the heck, you're always bringing stuff over to me," he said, thrusting a covered casserole dish at me. "And if you're gonna get well you need to eat. So here, I made you some soup."

"That's really nice. I don't know what to say."

"How about, 'Why don't you come in?' That works."

"Uh, sure. I'm kind of…uh, I don't know."

"No, don't worry, it's not like that. I'll only stay a minute, I promise. I know you want to get to bed."

Ono came out of the kitchen. "Everything okay out here?"

There was an ugly silence while everyone sized up the situation.

"Oh great," Hatch said. "Joke's on me, I guess. When you said you were going to bed early, I figured you were going there *alone*. Rookie mistake. My bad." He turned and rattled down the porch stairs as fast as I'd ever seen him move.

"Hatch!"

He threw a hand in the air, waving me off. There might have been a single finger salute in there, but it was getting too dark to tell.

"Hey, Pali, I didn't know," said Ono. "I've been accused of a lot of things, but horning in on another guy's territory isn't one of them."

"*Another guy's territory?* Really? What do you think I am, a tree that's been peed on?"

"No, that didn't come out right," he laced his fingers together and cracked the knuckles. "I guess I better go."

"You don't need to leave. Hatch was out of line just showing up like that."

"Yeah, well, whatever."

He grabbed the doorknob.

"*Mahalo* for going up there with me today," I said. "And I really appreciate the chopper ride, too."

"No worries. That's what friends are for."

He dashed out the door and clattered down the stairs almost as quickly as Hatch.

I sat in the shadowy living room, too spun out to turn on the TV or even a light. What a couple of weeks it'd been: first realizing that Crystal had disappeared, then Wong lying and threatening me, and Keith and Nicole vanishing and leaving me holding a wad of drug-infused cash. Then, in just the last twenty-four hours, I'd lost track of the only witness to Crystal's vicious murder, and I'd actually witnessed her bullet-ridden body. And, as if that weren't enough, I'd managed to run off the only two guys who'd shown any interest in me in ages. Detective Glen Wong might be a dirty cop, but there was no doubt in my mind I should've taken his advice and stayed completely out of it. Would've saved me a ton of heartache.

I waited an hour before I called Hatch. Time for him to cool off, and time for me to figure out how to 'fess up and make amends. Sure I was attracted to Ono, but he walked a tougher stretch of town than I was used to.

Hatch's phone rang once and went directly to voicemail.

I left a message. "Hatch, I'm really sorry about what happened. I should have told you I had plans. Please call so I can explain."

When he hadn't called by eleven o'clock I went to bed. I tossed and turned. The last time I looked, the clock said it was just after one in the morning.

I was half-dozing when I heard the creak of the hinge on the front door. I'd forgotten to lock it. I wasn't concerned, though, because it was just Steve coming home from the bar. He usually parked his car in the garage and came in through the back, but sometimes when he'd been out this late drinking he was smart enough to ask for a ride from a designated driver. I flipped my pillow over to the cool side and blissfully drifted back to sleep, glad to have him home.

***

I felt a presence in the room even before I was awake enough to see anything. Steve? No, it was someone else. And then there was the odor. Like a hand over my mouth, the smell enveloped me—overpowering the clean scent of sheets and pillow.

My eyes came into focus and there was Beni, standing over me with his stringy, clumped hair falling on either side of his face like a half-opened curtain.

"Hey, *wahine*, guess what? You sold me out," he hissed. "Now you pay."

I wasn't worried. Regardless of his threat, we both knew I could take him down in three moves.

"Get the hell out of here, Beni," I said. "I told you before if you pulled this stunt again, I'd lay you out like a prayer rug." I propped myself up on one elbow.

In the dusky glow of a three-quarter moon, the glint of something shiny was impossible to miss. It was a gun. A really big gun. And it was pointed right at my face.

# 31

Odd questions ran through my head as I stared at the business end of Beni's gun. Where had he been the last eighteen hours? How had a loser like him come up with such an impressive piece of weaponry? Did he know that in Hawaii a former felon like Beni could get tossed back into prison for even being in the same room as a gun like that? And, why was this fool pointing a gun at *me*—the person who'd fed and sheltered him when he had nowhere else to go? I don't scare easily, but guns—especially a gun held by a loose cannon like Beni—scare me. I'd been trained to mask fear, though, so I went with my best bluff.

"Beni, what the hell are you doing? Put that thing away."

"You don't like it when the guy you screwed over screws with you, right?"

"What are you talking about?"

"Oh yeah, you don't think I know you ratted me out to that cop? You play like you're gonna help me, and then you go to the cops to rat me out?"

"Beni, I didn't rat you out—to anybody."

"Liar!" He screamed. I hoped Steve heard and was upstairs calling nine-one-one.

"Look, Beni, put down the gun so we can talk. I never mentioned your name to the cops. And, after what I found out today, I'm pretty sure you're right—I think the cops were in on it."

"In on what? You trying to mess with me? No more talking. Get your ass outta that bed 'cuz we're going for a little ride."

"Okay, okay. Where do you want to go?" I slipped out of bed, holding a pillow to cover up as much as I could since I was only wearing an oversized tee-shirt.

"You're taking me down to Lahaina. Then we're gonna see about getting me the hell off this rock. If you make a call, or try anything stupid, I'm blowing your head off. I mean it. I done it before."

His hands were trembling. He transferred the gun from his right hand to his left while he wiped his palm on his shorts. Then he switched it back.

"Beni, listen to me. I believe you about what happened up in 'Iao Valley. I went up there today. And I know the Maui cops aren't to be trusted. I'm on your side."

"Shut up and get some clothes on."

I pulled on the same pair of shorts I'd worn all day. My rubber *slippas* were by the door. I assessed the situation and determined I could still probably drop Beni in three moves, but he was brandishing a Desert Eagle—one of the most powerful handguns on the planet. One small slip-up and one of us would die. The Chuck Norris moves would have to wait.

We trudged out to my car and by then Beni was carrying the gun down by his side. No doubt he'd used up most of his paltry upper body strength by waving the five-pound gun in my face for the past few minutes.

As I was getting into the Geo I noticed Steve had left the garage door open—something he never did. Also, it was empty.

"Beni, how'd you get into my house?"

"Walked right in. You so dumb you don't lock the door. You should be glad I got here first. The guys who're after me woulda popped you right there in your bed."

"Did you open the garage door?"

"Yeah, I woulda taken that little black car, but it was gone."

"You don't have a key."

"Don't need no key when you got skills."

"Why didn't you take my car?"

"This piece of *kukae*? No offense or nothin' but this car's garbage. 'Sides, I don't do no stick shift." He paused for a beat. "Enough yak. Take me to the harbor."

"Ma'alaea?"

"You deaf? I tol' you Lahaina. We're going to Lahaina Harbor."

I drove the speed limit. Not fast, but not too slow either. I didn't want to risk getting pulled over by Maui's finest while chauffeuring Beni and his five-pound pistol. I had a million questions, but I held off. The gun was in his lap, his right hand tensing on the grip. Every few minutes, he'd lift the barrel a few inches to remind me who was really in the driver's seat.

"Can we talk about that girl who got shot up in 'Iao?" I said.

"What's to talk about?"

"You haven't told me all of it, have you?"

"What you wanna know? She turned out to be more trouble than she was worth."

"Because the guy wouldn't pay the ransom?"

"Yeah, and some other stuff."

"Like...?"

"Like I don't want to talk about it no more."

We came out of the turns on the Pali Highway and dropped down to the flatlands heading toward Launiupoko Beach. Funny, only twelve hours earlier I'd seen this same beach from the air. It looked a lot prettier when I was sitting alongside Ono in the helicopter than it did in the dark of night with Beni poking a gun in my ribs.

"I feel kinda bad," he said breaking the silence.

"Bad about what? About dragging me out of bed in the middle of the night, or bad about threatening to blow my head off?"

"Nah, not that. I feel bad I had to shoot her."

My hands gripped the wheel as if someone had zapped me with a couple hundred volts.

"What're you talking about?"

"See this gun? It's not mine. That's why those guys are pissed. I took off with their fancy gun."

"You killed somebody Beni?"

"I guess."

"With that gun?" I glanced down at the glint of chrome.

"Looks that way."

"You know, the police have me under surveillance," I said. "They're probably following us right now."

Beni twisted in his seat. "I don' see nobody back there."

I took a glimpse at the rearview mirror. Black, nothing but black. No headlights and certainly no flashing blue lights.

"You think the cops been following you, eh? Did you ever think maybe it wasn't cops? Way I heard it, people I know been following you too."

I kept quiet.

"Spook you, eh? Now you know how I feel—everybody comin' after me."

"Can it, okay Beni? I need to concentrate on my driving."

We zipped down the dark highway. I tried to think of some way to attract attention but I'd never seen the island roads so empty.

"Okay, we're getting close to Lahaina." I finally said. "Where do you want me to turn?"

"Man, you musta got that old timer's disease or something. You can't remember nothin'. I said, take me to the harbor."

I turned left at Shaw, went a couple of blocks up Front Street, then turned and parked on Harbor Avenue. In the daytime, the area bustled with traffic and tourists. But in the dead of night it was just that—dead. I set the parking brake and waited for Beni to get out.

"Okay," he said, bringing the gun up to my temple. "Get out—slow. You and me are gonna go visit a friend."

"What friend? Who's expecting you at this time of night?"

"Oh, not a friend of mine—a friend of yours. Some guys told me about that dude you been hanging with. You know, your boyfriend with the catamaran, eh? He's gonna take me away from here. Otherwise, he's gonna watch his brand new girlfriend end up like that red-haired girl. Now move."

I got out of the car and assessed how I could turn the tables. In the dark, on the uneven footing of the dock, all I had to do was deliver one well-placed roundhouse kick. He'd go sprawling and more than likely the gun would skitter off into the drink. But then, if I missed...

"I know what you're thinkin' but I wouldn't try nothin' if I was you," he said. "I got friends here too. And they'd love a reason to get their hands on your buddy's boat. You mess with me, they mess with him."

I stopped abruptly. "Beni, I can't do this. You're going to have to shoot me. I refuse to take you down to Ono's boat."

"Listen to you. Looks like that black belt stuff knocked your brain *pupule.* You get movin' or I'll start shootin'. I'm not kiddin'."

I crossed my arms. He took a step back and gripped the pistol with both hands. Even so, his arms sagged under the weight of the gun. I had only a couple of seconds to react, but that was enough time to reach out and grip his right forearm, pull him crashing to his knees, and deliver a quick blow to his solar plexus.

The gun went off. I'm not sure if he purposely pulled the trigger or if it fired as a result of his finger contracting when I knocked the wind out of him. The blast boomed and echoed across the sleeping harbor so long it sounded like he'd emptied the entire magazine. The single round went airborne—straight up. What goes up must come down, but after a couple of seconds I was reasonably certain it'd landed somewhere other than my skull.

Lights flicked on in boat cabins and heads popped up from below decks.

I yanked the gun from Beni's limp hand and stood over him, waiting for possible retaliation from the drug dealers in the tricked-up yacht parked nearby. It was in the first slip—the one they'd stolen from Ono. But no one came up from the yacht. They didn't even turn on a light.

A plain vanilla cop car with a flashing cherry on the roof showed up within minutes. Three guesses who was first on the scene.

# 32

Detective Glen Wong, with his partner in tow, skittered down the dock with service weapons drawn. If he'd been behind the whole operation from the get-go, it couldn't have played out any better for him. There I was, holding a take-no-prisoners Desert Eagle chrome handgun, standing over a skinny dude I'd walloped into a near coma.

"Ms. Moon," said Wong as he approached. "Why does this feel like déjà vu all over again?"

"Before you get the wrong idea, Detective, I really need you to hear me out."

"You know, there's not much you could say that would change my mind," he said. "I told you no more than eight hours ago that if you didn't back off I'd throw you in jail. But here you are."

Ono came running down the dock from the other direction and Wong's partner stepped over and held out an arm to prevent him from coming any closer.

"She's a friend of mine," Ono said, as if our acquaintance would make any difference.

"We're taking her in," the partner said. "You can talk to her after she gets processed."

The paramedics arrived and bundled Beni up for the long ride back across the island to the hospital in Wailuku. The crowd on the wharf had grown to a couple dozen people. I flinched when somebody took my picture with a flash.

Wong nodded at his partner and Bert Konomanu went over and talked to the picture taker.

"Too bad you won't get to be on the news," said Wong as he ordered me to put my hands behind my back so he could snap on the handcuffs. "We don't reward vigilante behavior."

He escorted me back to the Fairlane and even put his hand on my head to make me duck down to slip into the back seat. I thought that was just something cops did on TV.

"You okay back there?"

"Never better," I mumbled.

We rode to the police station in silence. During the forty-minute ride I had plenty of time to mentally flip through a bunch of questions I knew would never get answered. How had Wong shown up at the harbor so quickly—especially since I hadn't seen him following me? Why was I being arrested before I'd been read my Miranda rights? And why hadn't I kicked Beni's ass when he was in my bedroom? I could've claimed self-defense and saved myself and the taxpayers of Hawaii a helluva lot of trouble and money.

When we got to Wailuku, Wong didn't take me in through the jail entrance but instead used a back door into a hallway I hadn't been in before. Great. I'd seen enough crooked cop movies to know this is how it goes: they throw you in an unmarked back room and say you resisted arrest or something. Then they hammer you down until you confess to some bogus charge.

"Do you want anything to drink? Coffee? Soda?" he said. We walked the full length of the hall before he ushered me into the last room and flicked on the light switch.

"No, *mahalo.*" If I was polite maybe he'd feel at least a little remorse over what he was about to do.

"You know why you're here?" he said. He gestured for me to turn around so he could take the cuffs off before I sat down.

"Obstruction of justice, harboring a known fugitive, and probably a bunch of other stuff you're gonna make up."

He shook his head. "I'm not going to be taping this interview, Ms. Moon. In fact, this interview never happened. I know you have a tough time with authority, and you're just bad-ass lousy at obeying orders, but I'm going to try again anyway. It's my job."

It pained me to hear him refer to his job as if he were Tom Selleck in *Blue Bloods*. Wong was a crooked cop, a guy on the take. He and his kind were a blight on the Maui Police Department and every other police department where cops step over the line and decide the rules don't apply to them. I wasn't going to give him any excuse to inflict physical pain, but I wasn't going to blithely go along with his self-serving BS, either.

"Yeah, whatever, Wong."

"The reason this interview never happened is because you're in a world of hurt. I'd hoped to spare you the really nasty fallout, but you insisted on bulling ahead. Now, I gotta figure out what to do with you. If I release you, you're a dead girl walking."

I didn't follow what he was saying.

"Are you threatening to *kill* me?"

He shook his head. "We're not the threat. You're now well-known by a group of thugs who have murdered at least five people—four of them women—here in the islands. They're associated with a drug cartel operating out of Southern California and Northern Mexico. The couple you were doing the wedding for...," he looked at me as if he was waiting for me to fill in the names.

"You mean Keith Lewis and Nicole Johnson?"

"Yeah, well those were the aliases they were using here in Hawaii. Turns out they're major players in a money laundering scheme for the Gato Negro drug cartel in Northern Mexico. Drugs are sold in the U.S. for American dollars. Then those dollars are used by our buddy 'Keith Lewis' to buy expensive real estate in Southern California. He turns around and resells the properties at a discount to get a quick sale and then deposits the proceeds in a bank account held by the cartel." Wong stopped, giving me a few moments to put the puzzle pieces together for myself.

"Anyway," he went on, "it's a great way to move large amounts of cash without throwing up red flags. Problem was, your guy got greedy. Wanted more than his fat real estate commissions. Our inside guy learned 'Lewis' pocketed over a half-million bucks that should have gone to his boss, one Juan Carlos Cardoza-Jimenez—head of the cartel. The middleman who'd recommended 'Lewis' to Señor C-J couldn't 'fess up that the guy he'd stood up for had bilked the boss. So, he came up with a way to force Lewis to give back the dough. He dreamed up a kidnapping, setting the ransom at the same amount Lewis had stolen. That way, he'd tip off 'Lewis' that he was on to him, and he could replace the boss' money and make things square before heads rolled."

"How do you know all this?" I said.

"Like I said, we got someone on the inside." He scratched the side of his head in a *where was I?* gesture. "But it didn't exactly go as planned. Seems when Lewis got wind of the ransom demand he thought it had come from the big guy himself—Cardoza-Jimenez. Which meant his life expectancy was down to days, maybe hours. So he throws the little bridesmaid under the bus and hightails it outta here."

"But that doesn't explain why you didn't investigate Crystal Wilson's disappearance. Why'd you stonewall me? Maybe we could've found her before they killed her."

"You have no idea how hard we all worked on this. I spent a fortune the department doesn't have on snitches and surveillance. We came up short."

"But why not tell the public? Don't you remember the Elizabeth Smart case in Utah? She was spotted by an everyday citizen on a downtown street. Why didn't you use the media—get the word out?"

Wong pinched his lips into a tight line. "I wish I could've. Unfortunately, I wasn't calling the shots here. It was the feds."

"Okay, now I'm even more confused."

"That bridesmaid—what was her name?"

"Crystal Wilson."

"Yeah, well, that wasn't her real name. She was an undercover agent for the Secret Service, planted at your bride's health club to befriend her. The feds had figured out the money laundering scheme and were ready to pounce, but they needed evidence. They sent your girl in to get something that would hold up in a U.S. court. We weren't getting much cooperation from the other side of the border."

"When she was grabbed, do you think the kidnappers realized she was a federal agent?"

"We're not certain, but from what we hear, we think they didn't know."

"Well, I know who pulled the trigger. He confessed to me. I can—"

"*Mahalo*, but we'll take it from here, Ms. Moon. This thing's already gotten ugly enough."

"I'm stunned. The U.S. government was willing to sacrifice a highly-trained Secret Service agent just to get evidence on a money laundering scheme?"

"This is big, Ms. Moon. It's the war on drugs."

"For the Secret Service agent it wasn't a war—it was an ambush."

***

I left the police station in a cop car. Wong told me I had two hours to 'get my affairs in order' and then I'd be relocated to a safe place until I could be called to testify before a federal grand jury. No telling how long that might take.

Two hours wasn't nearly long enough to say the good-byes I needed to say, or explain why I wasn't going to keep the commitments I'd made—like showing up at Sifu Doug's kung fu promotion ceremony later that day. But then, Crystal Wilson— or whatever her name really was—didn't even get two minutes.

We pulled up in front of my house and I went inside to pack.

# 33

I pulled out a dresser drawer and dumped a tangle of under-wear onto my bed. How could I just up and leave? I had two weddings next month. I couldn't just disappear. My friends would alert the media, put up a reward and generally make Wong's life miserable if he stonewalled them.

I called Wong's cell. "This isn't going to work," I said.

"It will. We already have a story for you. You're going to the mainland to put on a big wedding. Tell your roommate and it will be common knowledge before noon."

At five a.m. I knocked on Steve's door.

"You awake?" I said.

"I am now. What's going on? You've been crashing around for an hour."

"I've got to leave. I got a call from a guy in Las Vegas. Big-bucks, but totally off-the-radar. He wants me to do a fantasy wedding for his latest showgirl trophy wife but it's gotta happen fast. I'm leaving this morning."

Steve bolted upright in bed. "What? That's nuts. Don't you have two weddings already on the books? How're you gonna do them all?"

"I'm handing those over to Maui Dream Weddings. This one's way bigger."

"Pali, something weird's going on. Is it Beni?"

"It's not Beni, and nothing's weird. I just got a late-night call. I've gotta go." I crossed the room and kissed his forehead. "Tell everyone I'll be back as soon as I can. Hopefully no more than a couple of weeks."

"Aren't you going to call me when you get there?"

"I might be too busy. Don't worry. I'll tell you all about it when I get back." I headed for the door.

"Pali Moon, stop right there. You aren't leaving this house without telling me what the hell is going on." By now he'd gotten out of bed and was following me.

"I can't. Look, you know I love you and I'd stop and chat if I could. But I can't."

I started downstairs and then turned and looked him full in the face. We stared at each other for a few moments. Then a flicker of understanding flashed across Steve's face. "Got it. I'll let everyone know you were suddenly called away. But do me a favor, okay?"

"If I can."

"Stay safe. Las Vegas has got some pretty rough characters."

"Yeah, well so does Maui." I said.

He nodded.

I finished packing and then wrote a quick note to Farrah explaining that I was leaving but I'd be back as soon as I could. I left the note on the kitchen table. Steve would deliver it along with the news of my good fortune in being hired to do a lavish wedding for a Las Vegas high-roller.

I dragged my suitcase with the gimpy wheel over to the front door. There was an unmarked cop car waiting for me two doors down. As I hefted my suitcase down the porch stairs I looked back at my little house. I'd always considered buying that house my greatest achievement. Better than making black belt or graduating from college. The thought of never seeing it again made me falter on the stairs.

I looked up. A ghost of a moon clung to the edge of the sky. And in the east, the sun was just starting to smudge the horizon with the promise of a new day.

# EPILOGUE

On a rainy November day, Agent Elizabeth Stanton Collins was quietly buried in a full honors ceremony at Arlington National Cemetery. Her name was chiseled into the marble wall of a federal law-enforcement building somewhere in downtown Washington DC, but I'll bet that's cold comfort to her family and friends.

Beni Kanekoa folded like a cheap card-table and confessed to killing Agent Collins. He claimed he'd shot her under duress from drug dealers he owed a 'whole bunch of money' to. Not that the judge adjudicating the case gave a damn about Beni's claim of duress. In the end, Beni was sentenced to a life sentence without possibility of parole for murder while in the commission of another felony—kidnapping. Nothing was said in the State's case about Agent Collins being a federal law enforcement agent killed in the line of duty, since the federal case was still under wraps. At trial, Beni did step up and do the right thing by giving testimony to the victim's bravery and poise, even in the face of death. Again, cold comfort to her family and friends, but her legacy became an unspoken inspiration to those still fighting undercover in the seemingly never-ending war on drugs. It must be tough to keep up morale when you're battling a sadistic opponent with unlimited means.

And me? Well, I learned that Hatch's former fiancée was, in fact, murdered by the same cartel that murdered Agent Collins, so he'd been right in begging me to back off. Not that I've had a chance to talk to him about it. Until the feds are finished with their money laundering investigation and are ready to bring charges, I'm in limbo. I'm living under an assumed name—which is kind of ironic since the name I normally use is also assumed—in an undisclosed location known only to the fine folks in the Federal Witness Protection Program.

I'd like to give you a hint of what's going on, but I've been told if I plan to stay alive until the grand jury convenes, the less said the better.

Acknowledgements: Every author knows that although writing is a solitary job, you can't do it alone. A big shout-out to my review team: Diana Paul, Tom Haberer, and Jackie Edwards (aka mystery writer Nora Barker) for asking the right questions and catching the errors. Also, *mahalo* to my Facebook friends and fans who write reviews, especially: Rebecca Dahlke, Susan Cook-Goodwin, Wendy Lester, Linda Rosecrans Mitchell, Diana Paul, Kaye Haberer, and Denise Roessle.

Look for other titles in "The Islands of Aloha Mystery" Series:

*Aloha!*

Manufactured by Amazon.ca
Bolton, ON

11603790R00160